Philip Laundy - Best wishes
Alan — for a speedy
recovery.   18/3/89

Get Well!
    See you at home ... soon!

Allan
enjoy peace & good
health.
          [signature]

[signature]

Alan,
    I'll not forget
Tue. evening. Get well
fast. Come home soon.
Thanks for your friendship.
          Stephen

Barbara Reynolds

All the best
Ann Lewis

Best wishes Alan
Margaret Mitchell

Please, get well soon,
I may need you.
Best Regards.
Marcel-Roma.

Maurice se joint à moi
pour vous souhaiter un
prompt rétablissement
          Suzanne Duplessis

We missed your company
& hope you are well soon

Harry & Dorett
Brightwell

Alan, the fact that you did
not enjoy our company,
did you have to admit yourself
in an hospital? In all
seriousness get well soon,
          Peter & Teresa Boon

艾伦：
    祝您早日康复。
          李

Alan.
We expect to see
you in London — in
blooming good health!
          Joan Brennan

Corvina

Éva Kovács and Zsuzsa Lovag

THE HUNGARIAN CROWN

and Other Regalia

TITLE OF THE ORIGINAL:
A MAGYAR KORONÁZÁSI JELVÉNYEK
CORVINA KIADÓ, BUDAPEST, 1980
TRANSLATED BY PÉTER BALABÁN
TRANSLATION REVISED BY MARY AND ANDRÁS BOROS-KAZAI
PHOTOGRAPHS BY KÁROLY SZELÉNYI
DRAWINGS BY GÁBOR ATTALAI
DESIGN BY ISTVÁN FARAGÓ
JACKET BY ZSUZSA MEZŐ

SECOND, REVISED AND ENLARGED EDITION
© ÉVA KOVÁCS AND ZSUZSA LOVAG, 1980
ISBN 963 13 2298 X

CONTENTS

THE HISTORY
OF THE CORONATION INSIGNIA

Coronation as the act symbolizing the assumption of royal power became generally accepted in medieval Europe. The ceremonies that were performed in the various countries and which became traditional differed in their details and underwent changes in the course of time; yet their main features were identical. The indispensable elements of each coronation were the anointment with holy oil, the acceptance of the symbols of authority, the enthronement and the taking of the royal oath pledging to maintain peace and the rule of law. The ceremony was essentially a religious one, and the exact order of the presentation of the insignia, the prayers to be recited and the songs to be sung, as well as the text of the oath, were prescribed in advance. Secular elements were also part of the ceremony, such as the act of knighting or the girding with the sword, and the custom preserved in Hungary throughout that, replying to the question put three times by the crowning prelate—or, later, by the Palatine—those present declared their approval of the king's person by acclamation.

The ensemble of the coronation insignia varied somewhat according to the origin of the ceremony and the period. In Hungary, in the era of its first kings, up to the middle of the eleventh century, a lance was among the insignia; later, however, no trace of this can be found. We know from historical sources that, at medieval coronations, the cross, the ring, the bracelet and the harness all figured as regalia just as did articles of clothing, such as shirts, sandals, stockings. Each of them had their significance, symbolizing the various elements of royal authority. At all times and everywhere, the most important insignia were the crown, the sceptre, the orb and the sword. To these must be added the mantle which had special significance in Hungary owing to the long-standing tradition that it was part of the legacy of St. Stephen, the founder of the Hungarian state.

The Hungarian coronation insignia constitute one of the best preserved ensembles of relics of medieval Europe. This can be attributed, principally, to the special ritualistic reverence bestowed by the Hungarian kings, and the nation as a whole, upon the crown in the first place, but also upon the other insignia.

According to general belief developed in the Middle Ages, the crown, the sceptre and the mantle date from the first centuries of the Hungarian kingdom, directly from St. Stephen. The orb and the sword were added later, but it is certain that they replaced insignia that had existed previously and had been lost. As shown by the royal portraits on coins and seals, the orb had been part of the ruler's insignia ever since the time of Stephen I, so that the orb left to us from the fourteenth century continues earlier traditions. The same applies to the sword, which dates from the beginning of the sixteenth century; but a similar one was found among the royal insignia in the grave of King Béla III, indicating that the sword certainly played an important part in the Hungarian coronation ceremony of the Middle Ages. The Norman sword with the bone hilt, kept in the treasury of the Prague Cathedral and termed "St. Stephen's sword" in a fourteenth-century inventory, might have been its earliest predecessor.

7

The coronation insignia acquired special importance in Hungarian history. According to national opinion, the coronation was valid only if performed with these traditional regalia, considered to be the legacy of Hungary's first king. These insignia became real national and historical relics as early as the Middle Ages, and are preserved and treated as such to this day.

On 1 January 1001, Stephen, son of Prince Géza, descendant of Árpád, the chieftain under whose leadership the Hungarians had conquered their country, was crowned king at Esztergom. For this act, signifying the foundation of the Christian Hungarian State, Stephen, through his envoys, asked for and received a crown from Rome, where the two main dignitaries of religious and secular power in Europe, namely Pope Sylvester II and Emperor of the Holy Roman Empire, Otto III, happened to be staying together at the time. Although the only authentic contemporary record—the chronicle of Thietmar, Bishop of Merseburg—stresses the role of the Emperor, it is probable that it was the Pope who sent the crown to Stephen, following a joint decision by himself and the Emperor. The first Hungarian source mentioning the dispatch of the crown is the St. Stephen Legend written around 1100 by Bishop Hartvik who attributed the crown exclusively to the Pope.

We know nothing about the physical appearance of the royal head-dress sent from Rome; contrary to long-standing belief, the crown that has come down to us contains no element of the one given to St. Stephen. Perhaps it resembled the diadem set with gems and provided with a pinnacle decoration of lilies that can be seen in King Stephen's portrait embroidered on the mantle.

In the period of the pretenders' struggle for the throne that ensued upon the death of Hungary's first king, the coronation insignia were scattered. Some historians (e.g. Györffy and Vajay) give credit to a letter written by Pope Gregory VII in 1074 according to which Emperor Henry III, after having vanquished the Hungarian King Samuel Aba in 1045, sent the crown and the lance he had captured to Rome. Others (e.g. Deér) consider this information given by the Pope thirty years after the event as a distortion serving political aims and propose that the crown remained in Hungary. Two historical facts seem to confirm the latter theory. Henry III, after his victory, had his protégé, Peter Orseolo, who had been driven from the Hungarian throne, crowned again, most probably with the crown handed down from Stephen. Three years later, the Hungarian King Andrew I entrusted Liutvin, Bishop of Bihar, to collect the scattered royal jewels for the coronation and the bishop complied with the royal order. Further, it is highly probable that, when Bishop Hartvik referred to Stephen's crown sent from Rome, the crown was actually still in Hungary.

According to information dating from the twelfth century, the coronation insignia were kept in the Cathedral of Székesfehérvár. In 1166, Patriarch Michael Anchialus, in his laudatory address to Byzantine Emperor Manuel Comnenus I, urged him to occupy Székesfehérvár and obtain the crown. This information in itself suggests the particular importance of the Hungarian crown, and this is confirmed by an exchange of letters in 1198 between the provost of Székesfehérvár and Pope Innocent III about the safety of the crown upon which the country's honour—"honor patriae"—depended. By that time, the general opinion was gaining ground that the validity of the coronation was subject to its being performed with that particular symbol. This is the only possible explanation for the following event that took place a few years later, in 1205. When Ladislas III's mother helped the crowned child-king flee abroad to safeguard him from her brother-in-law, later King Andrew II, she took the crown with her to insure her son's reign. Under threat of war, Andrew II demanded from the Austrian prince who was giving shelter to the refugees the return of the crown which was of vital importance to him also; the armies were ready to march when the child-king's sudden death resolved the situation.

The belief that the crown was irreplaceable and non-interchangeable originated from the conviction that it had been bequeathed by the Holy King, founder of the state, who had received it from the Pope. From the beginning of the thirteenth century on, references—based on Hartvik—to the sending of the crown and to the insignia deriving from Stephen became more and more frequent. The first source left to us calling it The Holy Crown dates from 1256; and this term, together with the designation "the holy king's crown", occurred several times in the second half of the thirteenth century.

The long rule of Andrew II and then of Béla IV, represented a period of comparative tranquillity in the history of the coronation insignia. Events that were of outstanding importance both for the crown and the research into insignia history occurred only after King Béla IV's death in 1270. In the last years of his life, Béla IV waged an embittered struggle against his eldest son, Stephen, later to rule as Stephen V, who had several times revolted against his father. The old king was supported in this fight by his eldest daughter, Princess Anne, and her sons. After her father's death, Anne sought refuge in the court of Bohemian King Ottakar II. According to an Austrian chronicle written shortly after the event, she took with her two golden crowns, a ruler's sceptre, golden dishes and other precious objects adorned with gems. According to another, later chronicle, these treasures had been entrusted to Princess Anne by her father in order that she should rescue them from the rebel son; therefore, Stephen V came to hate his sister. Besides these narrative sources, the peace treaty signed at Pozsony (now Bratislava, Czechoslovakia), which, in July 1271, put an end to the yearlong war between Stephen V and Ottakar II, also mentions the precious objects. In this document, the Hungarian king, on his own behalf and in the name of his successors, renounced the royal insignia—"de insigniis regalibus"—which had been taken to Bohemia by Princess Anne and included a crown, a sword, a saddle, jewels, golden dishes and other treasures.

Just as in the case of the events of 1045, here, too, the interpretation of historical data is extremely difficult. It is possible that the crown taken away by Princess Anne, together with other gems, the sceptre and the sword, was only one of the jewels in the royal family's treasury and not the royal emblem proper, the "Holy Crown". (This term, by the way, does not occur in the sources relating the event, although we do come across it in earlier documents and in other contexts.) The fact, however, that the peace treaty in question dealt with the precious objects in a separate paragraph, calling them "royal insignia", suggests more than just family jewels.

In the years that followed, the question of the treasures taken out of Hungary emerged several times at the negotiations between the two ruling houses. In 1272 war again broke out between Ottakar II and Ladislas IV, successor of Stephen V who had died unexpectedly. The Hungarians waged this struggle that dragged on for many years in alliance with Rudolf of Habsburg, German king, who had adopted Ladislas IV, a minor at the time. According to Austrian sources, it was for him that as late as 1276 Rudolf demanded the return of treasures taken to Bohemia by Princess Anne. Ottakar II, however, did not comply with Rudolf's demand in the years to come. As an explanation, according to a source dating from 1278, he claimed kinship ties to Ladislas IV, whose crown he was thus entitled to guard during the Hungarian king's minority. After the death of the

Bohemian king in the same year, Rudolf made a final attempt to recover the treasures *(clenodia)*

from the child Wenceslas' guardian, but his demand was again rejected. This is the last mention of the jewels that were taken to Bohemia.

In 1290, with the death of Ladislas IV, who left no heirs, the linear succession of the House of Árpád came to an end. Andrew III, a progeny from one of the collateral branches, ascended the throne. Of the many pretenders emerging, he was the only one who did not have the support of any of the powers in Europe. Although a grandchild of Andrew II, he was born of that particular son of the monarch whom the ruling branch never recognized as legitimate. In this situation —when both the security granted by impeccable origins and adequate dynastic connections were absent—the "genuineness" of the coronation insignia was an important factor of legitimacy. In his coronation manifesto, Andrew III pointed out several times that this installation had been performed with "St. Stephen's Crown", and, according to a gift-deed from the period, he bestowed a present upon the provost of Székesfehérvár for having protected the important symbol of power from the king's enemies.

The legitimacy-warranting power of Stephen's crown was even more evident after the death of the last male descendant of the Árpád dynasty. On 27 August 1301, the Bohemian Wenceslas, descendant of Béla IV on the female line, was crowned at Székesfehérvár with the "genuine" regalia. However, the Pope and some of the feudal lords in Hungary gave their support to Charles of Anjou, also related to the House of Árpád on the female line, and he was crowned at Esztergom in the same year with an "emergency" crown. In the face of the papal stand threatening Wenceslas with excommunication and the consolidation of the Hungarian pro-Anjou faction, it was only his installation with St. Stephen's crown that kept the young Bohemian monarch on Hungary's throne for a few more years. Finally, summoned by his father, he returned to Bohemia in 1304, together with the coronation insignia. In October 1305, he renounced the Hungarian throne in favour of Prince Otto of Bavaria and handed over to him the coronation insignia. According to the Illuminated Chronicle, a medieval manuscript dating to the middle of the fourteenth century, Otto carried the crown with him concealed in a small wooden cask, which on the way to Hungary fell from his horse's saddle and lay in the dust until its absence was noticed. Then the party turned back and found it. Otto and his entourage took this incident to be a favourable sign from heaven. Notwithstanding, his luck in Hungary did not last long; eighteen months after his coronation at Székesfehérvár, he was captured, in the summer of 1307, by Ladislas, Voivode of Transylvania, who at the same time seized the coronation insignia.

It is obvious from all this that the possession of Stephen's crown was one of the important factors in the struggle for power. Papal envoy Cardinal Gentilis did his best, in the interest of Rome's protégé, Charles of Anjou, to make up for the deficiency, i.e. the absence of the insignia in question. At a meeting in Buda held to elect the king, the Cardinal, quoting Hartvik, stressed that the principal value of the crown lay not in its having been handed down by King Stephen, but in its having been consecrated by the Pope who then sent it to the founder of Hungary. At the envoy's suggestion, the feudal lords resolved that, should the regalia not be returned within a specified period of time to the king's possession and to their permanent place of safekeeping, to Székesfehér-vár, then the too highly revered crown itself should be banned by the Church and deprived of its sacral power. Based on these ideological foundations, the Cardinal solemnly consecrated a new bejewelled crown with which Charles of Anjou was crowned—for the second time—in June 1309. However, his adherents had to realize that public opinion would not accept him as the country's sole and rightful ruler while he was not in possession of the crown worn by his predecessors. *10*

Under the threat of the most severe religious punishment, excommunication, the Voivode of Transylvania was forced to return the coronation insignia, so that on 20 August 1310—on Stephen's Day—Charles was crowned for the third and final time. Till the end of his rule, he did not part with the symbols of power acquired with so much difficulty; he even took them with him for a long sojourn to Naples, and otherwise kept them under guard at Visegrád, the new royal seat. They stayed there also under the reign of his son, Louis the Great, after whose death in 1382 it was inherited, for the first time in Hungarian history, by a woman, more precisely by Louis's 11-year-old daughter, Maria. Elizabeth, the young Queen's mother, was the country's *de facto* ruler during that period; she very shortly angered an important group of the barons and they retaliated by offering the throne to Charles II of Durazzo, King of Naples, the oldest progeny of the House of Anjou. Charles persuaded Maria to abdicate and, with the help of his followers, had himself crowned on 31 December 1385. Elizabeth, who was forced to attend the ceremony together with her daughter, did not resign herself to the setback and had the new king murdered. At this, a revolt broke out, in the course of which she was taken prisoner and then died. Maria again became queen and ruled together with the elected king, Sigismund of Luxemburg, who had been chosen by Louis the Great as his daughter's husband. Their reign was a period of permanent domestic and external strife. In 1401, a group of barons held Sigismund prisoner for quite a while. The opposition again turned to Naples for a king, and invited Ladislas of Naples, son of the murdered Charles II, to Hungary. And, strangely enough, the events of almost a century before repeated themselves. In order to fortify his position, Ladislas had himself crowned at Zára (now Zadar, Yugoslavia) in August 1403. True, the coronation was performed, in keeping with tradition, by the Archbishop of Esztergom, but only with an "emergency" crown, consecrated by the papal envoy. The immense significance of the "real" crown, and the power its possession entailed, was proved again. Sigismund hurried to Visegrád, where, by presenting the crown to the people, he proved that he was the real ruler of Hungary. After a defeat suffered at the hands of Sigismund's adherents, Ladislas of Naples withdrew from the country.

In the second half of Sigismund's rule, the crown was transferred from Visegrád to Buda, to the increasingly important capital, where, according to a charter dated 1434, it was safeguarded under royal seal in the treasury of the palace; later, it was temporarily committed to the charge of the Archbishop of Esztergom. It was from him that, after Sigismund's death in 1437, his son-in-law, Albert, the first Habsburg in Hungarian history, accepted the royal insignia. However, he had to make important concessions in order to have himself crowned. One of these was that the crown came under the supremacy of the Estates, and they kept it first at Esztergom, and later at Visegrád. The chest containing the regalia and the door of the chamber holding it were secured by the seal of the king, as well as by those of several prelates and barons. Under such circumstances events occurred which were perhaps the most adventurous in the crown's history—events copiously and vividly narrated for us by one of the protagonists.

On 27 October 1439, King Albert died unexpectedly. His wife was pregnant and knew that she could assure the succession for her new-born only by possession of the crown. After uncertain rumours began to circulate about the disappearance of the crown, the Queen, at the beginning of November, together with members of the royal council, forced open the chamber door, broke the seals on the chest and inspected the insignia. One of the persons present was Ilona Kottanner, the Queen's lady-in-waiting, who then described the happenings in her diary. After the inspection, the crown was transferred to a smaller box and, together with her own crown, the Queen placed it in her bedroom. A candle which was kept burning at night caused a fire in the chamber, and the velvet cushion under the crown was already ablaze when Mrs. Kottanner, who had hurried in from an adjoining room, succeeded in extinguishing the flames. The dangerous incident could not be kept secret, and the next day the royal council decided that the insignia must be transported back to their original place and the chest containing them secured by the council members' seals. Having failed to obtain the crown, the Queen began negotiations with the feudal barons about marrying their candidate, the Polish King Władisław, who was several years her junior. In the meantime, however, she did not renounce her original plan and instructed Mrs. Kottanner to bring her the crown from the citadel at Visegrád. The Queen awaited developments at Komárom, while her lady-in-waiting entered the citadel on the night of 20–21 February 1440. Helped by a servant and a soldier, Mrs. Kottanner broke the seals and removed the padlocks, constantly worrying about ghosts, afraid of being discovered and tortured by compunction. They burned the crown's case and smuggled the precious booty out of the citadel concealed in a cushion after Mrs. Kottanner had re-locked the chamber door with the Queen's seal. The crown arrived at Komárom just in time, for on 22 February, the Queen gave birth to a son, Ladislas. Upon news of the crown prince's birth, the leaders of the royal council including László Gara, chief keeper of the crown, arrived, unaware of the happenings at Visegrád. They were ready to crown Ladislas, whereupon the Queen asked Mrs. Kottanner to smuggle the crown back, but the lady-in-waiting refused to undertake the dangerous trip for a second time. The other insignia remained at Visegrád and were, in fact, not handed over by the Estates for the coronation held at Székesfehérvár on 15 May. Mrs. Kottanner hurriedly sewed garments for the infant out of one of Sigismund's old formal robes; however, the opposing faction used the absence of "St. Stephen's sword, sceptre, orb and patriarchal cross" to cast doubt on the validity of the investiture.

In the meantime, in March, the majority of the Estates' representatives elected Władisław king, and on 17 July he, too, was crowned. The ceremony was performed with the real insignia; only the crown was replaced by a golden diadem taken from one of St. Stephen's reliquaries. Even this particular emergency crown, though closely connected with the mortal remains of the holy king, founder of the state, could not adequately replace the real one; this is why, in a document issued on the day of the coronation, the people's right to elect the king was strongly emphasized. It was stressed, at the same time, that no efforts were to be spared to recover the crown.

Queen Elizabeth tried to exploit the advantage which possession of the genuine crown meant to her son. In an appeal addressed to the people of Transylvania, she called her adversary's crown false and those who made Władisław king, traitors. The struggle between Władisław and the ex-king's widow lasted two years; meanwhile, she committed her son together with the crown to the care of her relative, Emperor Frederick III. The Emperor kept Ladislas with him, despite the fact that, upon Władisław's death in 1444, the Estates of Hungary recognized the child-king as their ruler and considered the coronation performed in his infancy valid. It was only in 1452, as a result of an armed revolt, that Frederick released the Hungarian king, without, however, handing over the crown.

In the period between Władisław's death and Ladislas's release, János Hunyadi, a general who had acquired great popularity in the Turkish wars, was regent of the country, and remained lieutenant-governor and "captain of the land" even after Ladislas's return. After Hunyadi's death, however, the king, influenced by the anti-Hunyadi faction of noblemen, had the general's elder son, László, executed, and his younger son, Mátyás (later King Matthias Corvinus), imprisoned.

After László Hunyadi's treacherous execution, the outcry of the lesser nobility made King Ladislas flee the country. He first went to Vienna and then to Prague where he died unexpectedly in 1457. It is indicative of the general popularity of János Hunyadi, the heroic fighter against the Turks and outstanding statesman, that the Estates, assembled to elect their ruler, proclaimed his son, Matthias, king on 24 January 1458. Despite his unanimous election marked by popular enthusiasm, Matthias did not risk having himself crowned, in the absence of the crown, with some other insignia. In his first royal proclamation, the recovery of the crown was declared as one of his main endeavours, second only to the defence of the country's frontiers, and the Estates were given the same task. But Emperor Frederick, who had refused to hand over the crown even to his relative, Ladislas V, was planning to extend Habsburg rule over Hungary, and so thwarted all negotiations aimed at handing over the crown. However, as his adherents were repeatedly defeated by Matthias, he pledged, in the peace treaty of July 1463, to return the crown. The document did not mention the tremendous amount of money—80,000 gold florins—which he demanded in compensation, and which he indeed received by means of an extraordinary tax levied on the Hungarians. Just before the transfer, rumours circulated that the Emperor had a copy of the crown made in order to lead the Hungarian envoys astray. As the crown had been kept abroad for 23 years, very few people knew it well enough to try to identify it. Finally, old Lord Chief Justice László Pálóczy, younger brother of Sigismund's keeper of the crown, made the trip to Wiener Neustadt, and from a nearly imperceptible crack in one of the sapphires he identified the crown, beyond any doubt, as the real one. After the transfer the regalia were exhibited at Sopron for three days and were then ceremoniously carried to Buda where Matthias was crowned amidst splendid celebrations on 26 March 1464. The Diet held on that date determined, in its Act II, the method of safeguarding the crown, declaring its safety to be the affair of the entire nation and not just that of the king and a small group of oligarchs. The law that founded regulations concerning the safekeeping of the crown in modern times did not prevent Matthias from entrusting the job of guarding the emblems to his most faithful followers. This was the situation till the end of his life. When he died unexpectedly, the crown was with his illegitimate son, János Corvin, who handed it over to Władisław of the House of Jagiełło, the king elected by the Estates; in the coronation procession, János Corvin himself carried the crown before the new king. This legal provision for safeguarding the crown was adhered to only during the reign of Władisław, who was generally known to be a weak-willed ruler. Several of his statute-books dealt with the question of the crown. According to his laws, the crown had to be guarded at Visegrád, and two keepers of the crown, who were lay persons jointly chosen by the king and the Estates, were responsible for its safety.

Nothing significant happened to the coronation insignia, kept according to the law at Visegrád, up to the disastrous battle at Mohács in 1526. At the time of the catastrophe—King Louis II also lost his life in the battle—Péter Perényi and János Szapolyai were the elected keepers of the crown. Szapolyai, who had played an important part in putting down the peasant revolt of 1514 led by György Dózsa, had ambitions for the throne and was supported in his endeavours by the lesser nobility and part of the aristocracy. With Perényi's help he obtained the crown and had himself crowned at Székesfehérvár on 10 November 1526. György Szerémi, a somewhat unreliable contemporary given to malicious gossiping, described the ceremony in detail. His statement that the crown "began to revolve" on King John's head—a sign of his being unworthy of power because his hands were still bloody from the liquidation of the peasant army—has more to do with the nation's general disposition at the time than with historic reality. Perényi then had the regalia

13

transferred back to Visegrád, but shortly afterwards he allied himself with the opposing party led by the widowed queen and the Palatine, and readily delivered the treasures for the coronation of Ferdinand of Habsburg in November 1527. In 1529, already as Ferdinand's keeper of the crown, he fled from the invading Turkish armies, but was captured by one of Szapolyai's followers and extradited to Sultan Suleiman the Magnificent. The Sultan handed over the crown to King John—who had come to the Turkish camp to pay homage—and the king kept the crown in Transylvania till his death. His widow, Isabella, made peace with Ferdinand in 1551 and solemnly handed him the crown.

Throughout the rest of the century the coronation insignia were kept in the Habsburg treasury at Vienna and Prague and were brought to Pozsony (now Bratislava, Czechoslovakia), the new coronation seat, for the enthronement of the kings, but always for a few days only. A change came about when Archduke Matthias, younger brother of the feeble-minded King Rudolf, had persuaded the latter to relinquish power in his favour. The Hungarians supported Matthias, and they demanded in compensation that he again keep the symbols of sovereignty in Hungary. The crown was handed over by Rudolf in Prague on 14 June 1608. The coach drawn by six white horses which carried the crown to Matthias's camp was escorted by 300 Hungarian noblemen. At the coronation in Pozsony, those assembled saluted Matthias II as the man who had victoriously recovered the crown, and the Diet held subsequently resolved that the insignia should be guarded in the fortress of Pozsony.

Péter Révay, who was to become the author of the first study written about the crown, and who loyally followed the treasures through all vicissitudes, was elected keeper of the crown. He made his first trip with them in 1616 when Matthias's wife was to be crowned and the king insisted on taking the coronation mantle to Vienna. At first, Révay refused its delivery, but when the Diet consented, he himself accompanied this national relic to the Austrian capital and shortly brought it back to Pozsony. Three years later, when the armies of Gábor Bethlen, Prince of Transylvania, occupied Pozsony, Révay handed over the crown to him. In 1620, Bethlen, who had been victoriously forging ahead with his army, was elected King of Hungary by the Diet of Besztercebánya (now Banská Bystrica, Czechoslovakia), but, although in possession of the regalia, he refrained from having himself crowned. Péter Révay followed the Prince's camp, together with the crown, to Zólyom, Kassa, Eperjes (now Zvolen, Košice and Prešov, Czechoslovakia) and Ecsed, until finally, in the treaty of Nikolsburg signed in 1622, Bethlen renounced all claims to the Hungarian throne and returned the coronation insignia to Ferdinand II.

The crown left Pozsony on two other occasions in the course of the century. In 1644, it was carried for a short time to Győr to escape the invading armies of the Prince of Transylvania, György Rákóczi I; then, in 1683, the Turkish advance necessitated its removal to Vienna, Linz and Passau. However, as soon as the Turks were driven out of Hungary, the crown was taken back to Pozsony, its permanent residence.

In 1703, the fortress of Pozsony was struck by lightning and partially burned down. This served as a pretext for taking the crown to Vienna; the actual reason, however, may have been that Vienna dreaded the consequences of the war of independence led by Ferenc Rákóczi II. In 1707, when the Diet of Ónod proclaimed the dethronement of the Habsburgs, the crown was still in Vienna. It was taken back to Pozsony only in 1712, after the defeat of Rákóczi's war of independence. Subsequently, the Hungarian Diets several times renewed legislation according to which the coronation insignia could not be taken out of the country, and, until Joseph II, the Habsburg rulers actually abided by that law.

Joseph II, who had inherited the throne from his mother Maria Theresa, refused to have himself crowned; this is why, in Hungary, he was mocked as "the king with a hat". In 1784, indifferent to Hungarian laws and sentiments, he had the coronation insignia transported to Vienna and had them guarded, together with the other crowns of his empire, in the court treasury. On his deathbed, realizing that his enlightened absolutism and his policy of centralization had failed, he retracted almost all of his decrees and consented to the return of the crown to Hungary. The keepers of the crown took possession of the treasures on 17 February 1790 and transported them to Buda in a triumphal procession of splendid carriages, under the escort of Hungarian noblemen. Ringing of bells, artillery salvos, fireworks and thanksgiving services received the crown all over the country. The procession arrived in the Hungarian capital after a three-day journey; for another three days, the crown was on public display. Then it was deposited in the Castle of Buda. Shortly afterwards, it was carried to Pozsony for the coronation of Leopold II, but two years later his successor was crowned in Buda.

During the Napoleonic Wars, the coronation insignia were taken, for safety's sake, to Munkács (now Mukachevo, Soviet Union) in 1805, and to Gyöngyös and Eger in 1809, escorted by the keepers of the crown and by mounted troops of the counties on both occasions.

During the first phase of the 1848 Revolution, the crown remained in the Castle of Buda. In December 1848, however, when the government had to flee from the army of the Austrian General Windischgrätz, it was transported to Debrecen on a special train; from there, also following the government, it returned to Buda. In 1849, during the last phase of the War of Independence, the Minister of the Interior, Bertalan Szemere, took charge of the crown and, by carrying and guarding it everywhere in great secrecy, he did his best to preserve the national treasure that had increasingly become a troublesome burden amidst the general chaos. He took it first to Szeged, then to Arad, later to General Bem's camp at Lugos, and—when the Hungarian troops had capitulated—to Orsova (now Arad, Lugoj and Orşova, Rumania) where, assisted by a few of his trusted men, he buried it under an abandoned house. Afraid of having been spied upon, next day he returned and found the place disarranged, but the chest containing the insignia was intact. He found a new hiding-place in an isolated willow-grove on the river-bank. He and his men buried the chest and carefully covered up their traces. In emigration, Szemere shared his secret with a few more persons, and later it was one of them he suspected of treason. However, it was never ascertained who actually guided Austrian Colonel Karger to that willow-grove on the banks of the Danube. (The Colonel had been charged by the Viennese government with the task of tracking down the crown.) The chest was discovered in September 1853; it had become rusty in the ground, both outside and inside. The crown and the sceptre were intact in their separate cases, but the sword became rusty, the mantle entirely soaked and the sandals, stockings and other articles of clothing in the bottom of the chest had mouldered away. A warship took the precious find to Buda, where it was received by large crowds, artillery salvos and a thanksgiving service. Francis Joseph asked that the insignia be sent to Vienna for a day. He inspected them, and then returned them to Buda, where he—a king who had already been ruling for almost twenty years—was crowned in 1867.

The last coronation in Hungarian history—that of Charles IV—took place in Buda, too, in 1916. After the ruler was expelled from the country, the period of the "kingdom without a king", when

15

Regent Nicholas Horthy wielded power "in the name of the Holy Crown", lasted to the end of the Second World War. Even the Arrow-Cross "leader of the nation", Ferenc Szálasi, took an oath on the crown in November 1944 after his group of Nazi sympathizers seized power. When the battle-front was approaching Budapest, Szálasi and his entourage fled along with the insignia to Veszprém, Kőszeg and Velem; then, in March 1945, they, and the insignia, crossed the border. In the vicinity of Mattsee, a small village in Austria, several guardsmen entrusted with the task of safeguarding the crown buried the treasures in a barrel and turned over the crown's chest to the U.S. Army. Unaware of the fact that the chest was in fact empty, the U.S. Army guarded it for a few weeks at headquarters until, finally, one of the men who took part in the burying of the regalia disclosed their hiding-place. So the coronation insignia came under U.S. authority in June 1945.

During the years of the Cold War, the whereabouts of the Hungarian crown could only be guessed at. The first official statement that the crown was being kept in the U.S. treasury at Fort Knox, as the "special property" of the Hungarian people, was made in 1965.

As a result of reiterated demands by the Hungarian government and of international détente, Antal Apró, President of the National Assembly, on behalf of the Hungarian people, accepted the precious relics of Hungarian history from U.S. Secretary of State Cyrus Vance on 6 January 1978.

THE CORONATION INSIGNIA

The literature dealing with the Hungarian crown and the other regalia is copious and profuse. The first book on the subject was written by Péter Révay, keeper of the crown, and appeared in 1613; this work by the Lord Lieutenant of Turóc County ushered in the writing of art history in Hungary. Interest was always principally centred on the most important, and most disputed, piece of the ensemble, the crown. Besides the statements which have crystallized gradually and can now be treated as facts, there are many views in the literature that contradict and even exclude each other. There are several reasons for this. First of all, the legal and sacral significance, dating from the Middle Ages, of the regalia, and mainly of the crown, a significance which, under the impact of various political factors, has been distorted in the course of time, hindered, both in principle and practice, any unbiased scientific study. As a consequence, experts rarely had the opportunity to examine the objects, and if so, under inadequate circumstances and with inadequate methods only. Even in the cases in which the coronation insignia could be studied—twice in the nineteenth century and, within certain limitations, on several occasions in the twentieth—scholars were, unconsciously, inhibited by traditions; in one way or another, they tried to maintain the plausibility of the theory that the crown, termed holy and said to be derived from St. Stephen, had actually been in contact with the person of the first Christian king of Hungary.

Medieval tradition attributed to Charlemagne the German imperial crown presently in the Treasury in Vienna, even though it was made several centuries after his death. Emperor Charles IV proceeded in the same spirit when he commissioned the Bohemian royal crown specifically as an emblem of Wenceslas, the country's princely patron saint. The royal emblem served, at the same time, as the crown of the sacred relic. As far as the historical past of Hungary is concerned, the coronation insignia were always connected with St. Stephen's monumental figure; they were referred to as St. Stephen's mantle, St. Stephen's crown rightfully so, as the medieval way of thinking was not bound by any archaeological considerations. As for the mantle, tradition partially coincides with truth; as for the crown, even in the modern historian it stimulates tendencies similar to that of the medieval chronicler or legend-writer. And should it be outright impossible to identify any part of the crown with that of the one-time crown of the first Hungarian king, well then, let that part be a relic of St. Stephen's in some indirect way: perhaps the cross-band is a remnant of a book cover or any other object commissioned by the king, or the socket of his cranial relic, or the cross surmounting the crown a part of his (supposed) one-time orb.

In the absence of data, it is equally difficult to prove the role King Coloman or Béla III supposedly played in some phases of the history of the insignia. In the past, I too was inclined to prefer such solutions, although the concept itself is misleading; it is erroneous to suppose that only important historical personalities can play a part in the fate of important objects.

Returning to the study of the regalia, it was a paradoxical turn of events that gave new impulse and a somewhat new direction to research. Some experts had the opportunity in postwar Germany to thoroughly examine the relics which were practically inaccessible to Hungarian scholars. The insignia were studied by foreign experts less well versed in Hungarian history. This negative factor, together with personal research, had a positive effect: it contributed to the development of a more objective outlook. Thus, József Deér, the late professor at Berne University, Switzerland, based his great monograph about the crown on the observations of others (Boeckler, Wilm, Kelleher) and on the photographs taken at the time. His work, supported by vast research, is an indispensable foundation for any further study. It is Deér's lasting merit to have treated the historical problems connected with the insignia and to have surveyed such a wide range of possibilities, both as far as the questions of insignia history and art history are concerned, as nobody before him had.

Partially under the impact of the respect I felt for this work, based on sound scholarship, I referred in the past to Deér's work when writing about the crown. In publishing my own research, I was made wary by my earlier experience; just as Deér's book about the crown, my study about the coronation mantle was based on the observations of others. As opposed to Deér, Mrs. Magda Bárány-Oberschall consistently supported the view that is valid for every similar historical treatise, namely that the only reliable starting-point is the thorough and up-to-date examination of the objects themselves. The study of the objects *per se* does not supply answers to each and every question that may emerge, but it can lead to the discovery of such fundamental facts as can constitute the basis for further historical treatment.

The present modest work is based on the own studies of the authors; however, it was written before the complementary examination of the material, an examination both possible and necessary, was undertaken. The purpose of the present treatise is, first of all, to acquaint—partially by publishing new photographic material—interested readers with the objects themselves, with these, in many respects unique, precious relics of Hungarian history.

The Crown

It has been discovered fairly long ago that the Hungarian crown obtained its present form by the assembly of parts of two different crowns. This claim, considered valid for a long time, proposed that the upper part, consisting of the cross-band with inscriptions in Latin, was St. Stephen's ancient crown, a gift from Pope Sylvester II mentioned in Hartvik's legend. This was the *corona latina,* the Western crown. On the cloisonné plaques of the crown's lower part, there are Greek inscriptions, indicating that it must be a work of Greek or, more precisely, of Byzantine origin, coming from the Eastern Roman Empire *(corona graeca)*. The three portraits on this lower diadem represent historical lay personalities. Their identification was an achievement of the Age of Enlightenment, and is, to this day, the most solid fact in the history of the object. Those portrayed are Byzantine Emperor Michael Ducas, a Constantine born in purple and Hungarian King Géza. Michael Ducas is surely Michael VII and Géza—Géza I. The Constantine born in purple, i.e. as an emperor's son, must be either the Emperor's younger brother or his little son, co-emperor at the time. The reign of these three coincided, so the pictures must have been made between 1074 and 1077. The first obvious conclusion, namely that the crown had been donated by the Byzantine emperor shown in one of the pictures, to the king, also portrayed, was later replaced by the view, based on various considerations, mainly upon the crown's female type, that the diadem had been made for the queen and not the king.

The Byzantine Crown

18

The circlet of the Greek crown is an almost regular circular band, welded at the back, formed out of a fairly thick (1.5 mm.) gold plate, and having an inner circumference (63.6 cm) much greater than the perimeter of a normal human head. (Its outer circumference is 68.5 cm.) At the centre the band is surmounted, both on the obverse and on the reverse side, by a semicircular, protruding part. On the larger of these, coinciding with the front of the head, was placed the plaque showing the figure of the Pantocrator, while the Emperor's portrait figured on the smaller, back plaque, the Emperor being the other main protagonist of the ensemble. On the headband itself, square cloisonné enamels and precious stones alternate—eight each—so that the bigger gems are placed in the broader compartments below the protruding sections. The ornamental pinnacle decorations (four on both sides) of decreasing size and alternately in arch and gable form all have an *à jour* (translucent) enamel finish, and flank the enamel figuring Christ. Pierced gems are dowelled to their tops substituted by a pearl on the two outermost ones. The enamelled acroteria continue as a row of pearls mounted on pins on the reverse side and run to the protruding plaque at the back. Pendant chains hang from the lower rim of the circlet, a cluster of four on each side and with a single one at the rear.

The cloisonné enamels are the least mysterious parts of the crown. The ten plaques undoubtedly constitute a homogeneous series: the refined finish, the clarity of design, the clear and intelligent application of the traditional solutions and the splendidly balanced elegance of the enamel palette make it one of the finest ensembles of the genre. It ranks high even among the relics of the imperial workshop of Constantinople.

Around the enthroned Pantocrator (Christ, ruler of the world) represented on the largest plaque, the saints seem to form a sort of paradisiacal royal court. The paradisiacal site is indicated by the stylized cypresses rising on both sides of the throne. The archangels with multicoloured wings, wearing ornamental tunics and headbands in the Hellenic tradition and supplied with a herald's staff, are divine messengers. According to Gyula Moravcsik, the noted Byzantologist, they refer to the heavenly origin of royal power. Of the archangels, Michael is frequently represented as the divine bearer of princely insignia. Moravcsik's examples, taken mainly from literature and miniatures, can be complemented by others, e.g. by an enamel picture (Khakuli icon, Tbilisi Museum) and by a coin issued by Emperor Isaac II (Isaac Angelus). Another role awarded to Archangel Michael is that of the archistrategos, or the warrior leader of the heavenly hosts. In this case, however, the heavenly hosts are represented by another pair dressed in splendid armour and holding a shield and a spear: St. George, the soldiers' patron saint, and Demetrius of Thessalonica, the most venerated militant saint of Byzantium. Both were considered protectors of the Empire against the attacks by the barbarians, the infidels and the pagans. The archangels and soldier-saints shown as beardless youths are followed on the reverse side of the circlet by two half-length portraits of classic beauty: the more simply dressed figures of Cosmas and Damian, the two physicians who cured their patients free of charge. In Moravcsik's first interpretation, they represented selfless heavenly science. On the central enamel of the reverse side of the crown, with its back to the Pantocrator, is the Byzantine emperor occupying the peak of wordly hierarchy, "Michael the Ducas, Emperor of the Romans, believer in Christ"; to his right (left for the spectator) on the circlet is "Constantine, Emperor of the Romans, born in the Purple Palace", and on his left, "Géza, faithful [loyal] King of Turkia". (By Turkia Hungary is meant here.) The Byzantine rulers are round-faced with curly, dark hair. Emperor Michael has a full-beard and a drooping moustache; the youth's face is smooth. Their open *stemmas,* adorned with pendants, are

23

exactly alike, and both hold a *labarum,* or imperial military standard, in their right hands. In the other hand, the older man holds a sword, and the younger a consul's scroll. Their robes of state are versions of the imperial gala. Over the two richly adorned tunics, Emperor Michael has donned the *loros,* a kind of stole, decorated with gems and pearls; the younger man wears the tunic embellished with an ornamental collar *(maniakion).*

Before speaking about the portrait of the Hungarian king, it is worthwhile to deal with some questions touching upon the whole of the ensemble. Except for the details, everybody agrees that the enamel pictures represent heavenly and worldly hierarchy. The role of the physician saints is much debated. They are expressly the guarantors of the emperor's physical well-being. This is why Deér considers their present placement as erroneous. Belonging, as they do, to the group of worldly rulers, they would occupy the place suited to their high rank only if the portraits were reversed; they shouldn't look in Christ's direction, but in that of the emperor. Except for the two Byzantine rulers staring into the air, all the persons are looking somewhere: Christ to the left, the angels sideways and upward at Christ; the saints with a strange fixedness from the corner of their eyes also look towards Christ; and Géza looks at the emperors. The linking of the glances divides the pictures in two unequal groups representing celestial and earthly protagonists. According to Deér, however, two equal groups both consisting of five members should be taken into account. Despite the fact that in the structure of Byzantine ensembles, the direction of the glance of the figures does not point to a consistently applied rule of composition, specifically in the case of the *corona graeca* we may accept such a rule as applying to the original arrangement. The rearrangement of the groups is the result of special considerations. Since Boeckler's investigations, the majority of researchers exclude the possibility of Ducas' crown having been left to us in its original form. The original form has been visualized in a number of ways: a circlet with both the Pantocrator plaque and the Ducas plaque located on the band proper; a crown consisting of the enamels only, with the rows of pearls set between them (Boeckler); or a two-tier woman's diadem with the two semicircular shields one above the other in the middle and with ornaments on top, similar to the one worn by Byzantine Empress Irene-Piroska, daughter of Hungarian King St. Ladislas, in a mosaic picture of a later date (Hagia Sophia, Istanbul; Mrs. Bárány-Oberschall). Deér went even further: though he did not completely exclude the possibility, he considered it almost impossible that the enamels were originally meant to form the parts of any crown. In his opinion, they might have belonged to any object of an arcade-like composition adorned with plaques originally arranged in two equal groups. The conclusion drawn from Boeckler's observations form the basis of all these suppositions. It was Boeckler who established the fact that the material and workmanship of the cloisonné plaques were much finer than the individual elements of the otherwise homogeneous setting (fundament plate, beaded wire, dowels, the settings of the gems and the enamels); as for the enamelled acroteria, he referred to their workmanship as "barbarian". He asserted that the style and finish of the setting and of the *à jour* enamels were unworthy of Byzantine art. Deér partially modified Boeckler's view; according to him, the setting was in effect Byzantinizing and the diadem was of a Byzantine type. Hence his conclusion: the diadem, in its present-day form, was assembled in Hungary, but with a Byzantinizing intention, with the conscious utilization of the Byzantine figured plaques of an earlier date; the crown was made for Anne of Antioch, King Béla III's first wife. It is incomprehensible, in a way, how the otherwise excellent Boeckler could have referred precisely to the Byzantine liturgical vessels in the treasury of St. Mark's in Venice when trying to prove that the details of the *corona graeca* were alien to

Byzantine art. The clear, almost geometrically rigid division of the ornamental system with the help of the thick, plastic beaded wire, the alternation of gems and stones polished to a regular form, with the enamels, the frames made of rows of pearls strung on wire and dowelled—it is precisely here, in the unmatched Byzantine collection of the Venice treasury, that similarities in detail can be observed in great numbers. Examples of the simple, pronged setting of the stones can also be found here. The division of compartments into squares, with filigree threads, is exemplified by a tenth-century book cover (Treasury of the St. Athanasius monastery, Mount Athos). As for the "ugly, empty spaces" (Boeckler) surrounding the gems, there are, in fact, among the relics of Byzantine art, even more "extreme" examples of this than on the Hungarian crown band: the foot and the rim of an agate chalice, the setting of a heliotrope cameo representing Christ and the frame of a cloisonné enamel triptych (Ermitage, Leningrad), or the border of the paten in the Stoclet collection in Brussels. As a matter of fact, the finer the cloisonné enamel, the finer the gold it requires. Soft, pure gold is, however, less suitable and necessary for the setting which serves as structural support at the same time. Therefore, the fact that the plaques and the setting have different gold alloys is by no means paradoxical, for it can be a practical requirement. If we consider that, in other cases, only gilded silver was used in addition to golden cloisonné enamels, we may come to an opposite conclusion in judging the crown's supporting band. One of the fundamental points in Deér's claiming that the crown was made in Hungary during the reign of Béla III is the correspondence between the tri-lobed stone settings and the bezel in the ring found in the king's grave; and, as this motif does not occur anywhere else, it must be considered a speciality of the royal Hungarian workshop. As a matter of fact, this sort of setting is rare indeed, but by no means unique. In addition to an example from late antiquity, the setting of the ring owned by Jacques de Vitry, the one-time Patriarch of Antioch (1240), is of the same kind (Soeurs de Notre-Dame, Namur). Besides, Béla III's ring was widened, and it is possible that the robust king had not been its first owner (Györffy). As for the pinnacle decorations their evaluation from the point of view of art history is difficult, because their technique is unique indeed. To claim a Hungarian origin for them—placing them among the small group of Romanesque cloisonné enamels in Hungary, also of uncertain origin—is by no means a reassuring solution. What are we actually talking about here? About cloisonné enamels, which, however, have no gold base and are not placed on some supporting plaque either. Consequently, they are held together exclusively by the cloisons and the frames themselves; undoubtedly thicker wires are certainly more fitted to this purpose than wires thin as hair. Since the cloisons had to be soldered to one another and not to the base, the design is more exposed to distortions. The enamel fields are large; pollution accumulates in the enamel, producing blisters and making the surface uneven. The row of acroteria *(pinnae)* is not very attractive at first glance or in the photographs taken in the past, nor does it seem refined. Our aesthetic misgivings only disappear when we see the ornaments in radiating light shining through them. Then the blue and the green of the pattern of golden design sparkle in all their splendour, in harmony with their purpose. In both East and West, the feather ornament is a frequent accessory of the royal head-dress. The patterns of the peak ornaments must originate from this custom, the "fish-scale" decoration being in fact the stylized imitation of blue-green-and-gold peacock feathers. Their technique being complicated, it is easier to conceive them as the product of a Constantinople workshop of long-standing tradition than the unique invention of a twelfth-century Hungarian goldsmith. The home of the stylized feather ornament is Byzantium, too.

25 Closely related to the motif on the pinnacle ornaments are the "Byzantinizing" or probably

The enamels of the Byzantine Crown
represent heavenly and worldly hierarchy.
Above the forehead is Christ Enthroned,
on the bands, arranged in pairs,
are the half-length figures
of the Archangels Michael and Gabriel,
of SS. George and Demetrius
and of SS. Cosmas and Damian.
The representatives of worldly hierarchy
are shown in the rear part
of the crown. On the band:
Constantine Porphyrogenitus and King Géza of Hungary.
Above them, in the centre,
occupying the place of honour,
is the portrait of Emperor Michael Ducas.

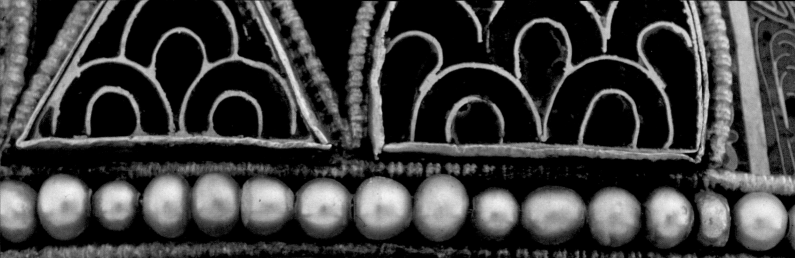

Ὁ ΔΗΜΗΤΡΙΟΣ

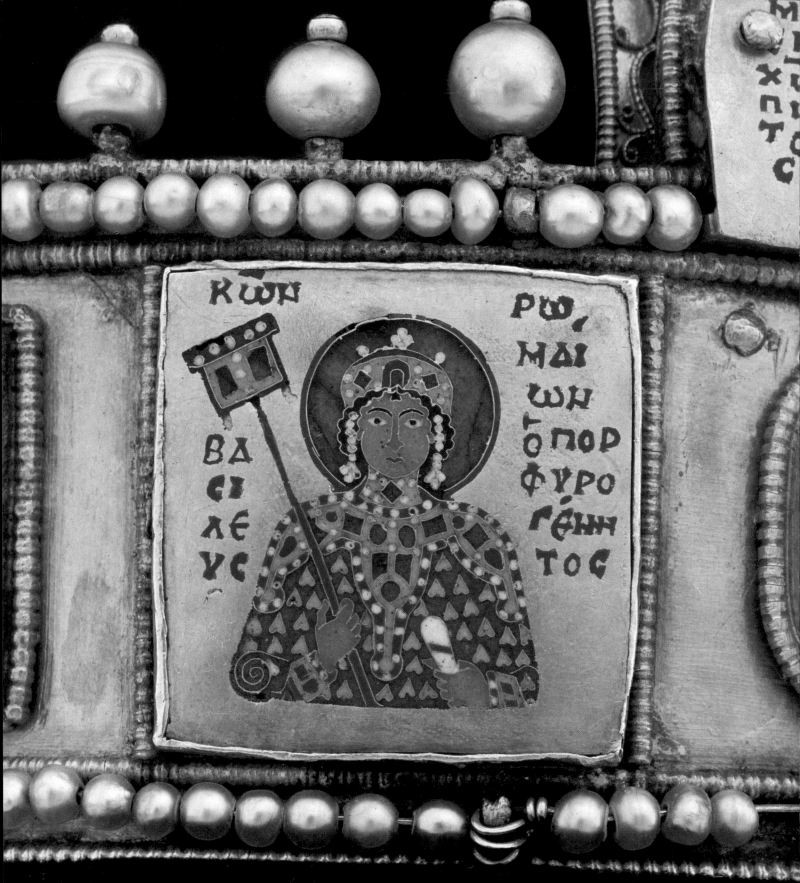

Byzantine fibulae with eagles which formed part of the Mainz jewel find (Altertumsmuseum, Mainz, resp. Kunstgewerbemuseum, Berlin).

So the *corona graeca* is an authentic Byzantine work indeed; apart from a few minor changes, all its details are contemporary with the cloisonné enamels. (The sapphire on the reverse side replaced an earlier, broken one during the reign of Matthias II; the Ducas plaque was moved downward and, for this reason, a section of the upper row of pearls serving as a frame was removed.) The pendants constitute a problem. The dowels of five of them are obviously of the same material as the other parts of the crown. Of the pendants two on both sides are suspended from rings hanging directly from the circlet. Furthermore, the pendants ending in tri-lobed palmettes are not exactly alike.

A few more words now about the gems which are not particularly precious. The green ones are made of glass. As a matter of fact, on early medieval objects one should not look for stones that are "good" from a present-day jeweller's point of view. It was their size and the alternating colour harmony that counted in fitting into the composition. Besides, gems of a regular shape were always given preference in Byzantium.

The question should be raised now whether Michael Ducas' gift was produced for the king or for the queen. In the uniform view of insignia historians, the pinnacle decorations are typical appurtenances of female crowns, but it should be mentioned that men's crowns with acroteria can also be found in illustrations. The description of the genesis of the Byzantine female crown is again Deér's achievement. It is into this series of crowns that he fitted the *corona graeca* (thought to be of Hungarian origin) by asserting that the crown of the Hungarian queen, ranking below the *basilissa,* is lower because of her lower rank (the crown of the Byzantine empress being a "tiered" one). It struck some researchers, most recently Györffy, that the head-dress of King Géza represented on the crown, if imagined without its acroteria and pendants, is quite similar in structure to the *corona graeca* itself. Elaborating along this line of thought, one could say that *with* pinnacle decorations and pendants, it is the "female" double of the *corona graeca*. The conclusion one can draw from illustrations is that the empress's crown was occasionally constructed on the basis of this principle.

The crown of Empresses Zoe and Theodora (diadem of Constantine Monomachus, 1042–1050, Hungarian National Museum, Budapest), that of Eudokia Makrembolitissa [?] (ivory carving, 1068–1071, Cabinet des Médailles, Paris) and Irene's head-dress (Pala d'Oro, pre-1105, St. Mark's, Venice) correspond exactly to the traditional shape of the Byzantine emperor's crown, with the sole difference that they have acroteria.

Accordingly, the Byzantine diadem having pinnacle decorations indicated the status of "the Queen of Turkia" in keeping with Byzantine protocol at least. It does not follow from this, however, that the Hungarian royal crown was exactly the same as that shown in the Byzantine picture. It is improbable that the maker of the enamels knew the Hungarian king's actual regalia. Even if he knew about them, we could not expect him to have presented them so realistically. What happened was that he translated the Hungarian king's rank into the peculiar language of the Byzantine pictures, in conformity with Constantinople protocol. Obviously, the Hungarian king could rank only below the Byzantine rulers: Géza stands in third place, behind the emperors who are surrounded by nimbi. His crown is narrower than the *stemma* of the emperors; it looks almost like the trimming on his dark cap. Below the broader band, the emperors wear a similar cap, made of red or blue material. The rigid hoops of the circlets were made more comfortable by the caps worn underneath; that is probably why the *corona graeca* was so large.

The Hungarian king's attire is also more modest. The simplicity of his tunic is particularly

The pinnacle decorations
of the Byzantine Crown
in translucent light.

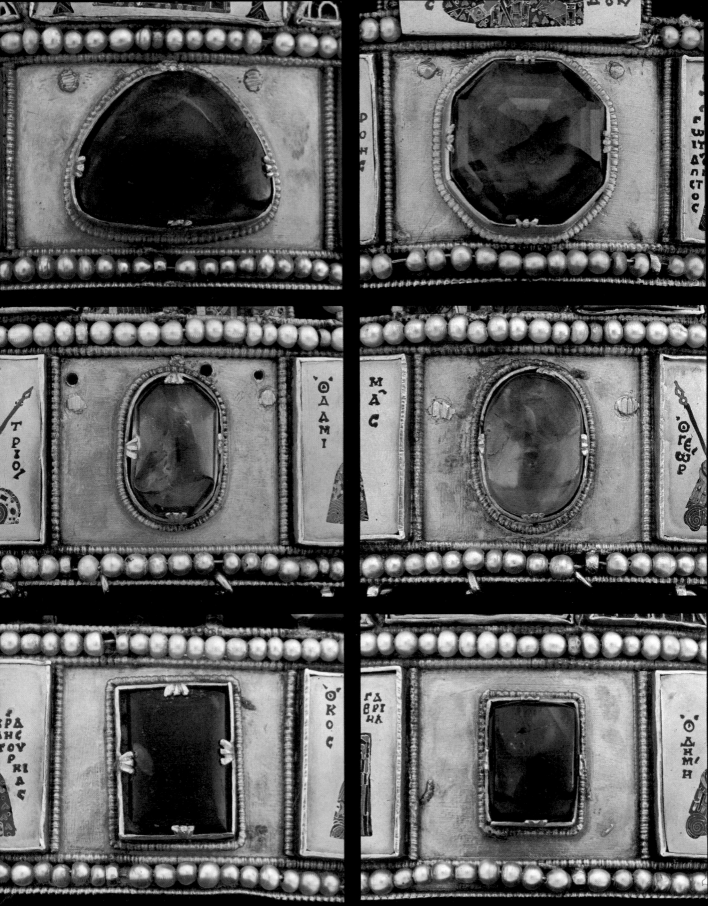

The outside
and inside
of the pendants
on the left.

noticeable. Nevertheless, his mantle *(chlamys)* made of patterned fabric and adorned with a *tablion,* a kind of decorative motif, occurs also in the pictures of the emperors. Just as Ducas, he holds a sword in his left hand, and an unusually shaped cross in his right. Géza's insignia were considered indicative of the fact that the Hungarian king had been placed on a relatively lower rung in the Byzantine hierarchy, i.e. among the "patricians". Not a word of this, however, appears in the inscription on the plaque which exactly defines the Hungarian king's status. As Moravcsik proved in his exemplary, classical analysis of the inscriptions on the crown, the inscriptions on the portraits of Byzantine rulers corresponded, both in form and content, to the signatures on imperial charters. The enamel is red because the charters had to be signed in purpled ink. Michael Ducas' name and title are abbreviated just as on the coins. The inscription on the Hungarian king's portrait is in blue enamel, his title corresponding to the one valid in Hungary in the eleventh century: *krales = király* (king) = *rex.* Moravcsik sees a certain tendentious ambiguity in the inscription; Géza's adjective *pistos* may mean "believer in Christ" but also "loyal to the Emperor". It is preferable to accept the former meaning. The abridged form of the expression "believer in Christ", occurring on the Byzantine coins beside the emperor's name, corresponds, in content, to the expression *Dei gratia* (by God's grace) added to the name of Western rulers and the Hungarian king as well. This is the meaning of the illustration. The Hungarian king does not hold a "patrician cross" *(Ankerkreuz)* in his hand, but rather the same emblem as Basilissa Maria, Michael Ducas' wife in the famous double portrait of the Khakuli icon which represents the royal couple's heavenly coronation. However, the two cannot have an identical insignia of rank. So that the meaning of the emblem must be different. There is a sceptre ending in a cross in both pictures. The tendrils below are the simplified forms of the lyriform palmette or ornamental foliage accompanying the cross designs. This is why they were—erroneously—believed to be patriarchal crosses, although in Géza's picture the red of the foliage differs from the blue of the cross.

There is no possibility here to acquaint the reader with the entangled story of this ancient motif. Suffice it to say that it refers to the wood of the cross, the cross relic. The cross is the instrument of salvation; Christ, by having vanquished death when dying on the cross, changed it into a weapon triumphant over the enemy. This weapon is the main guarantee of the defence of the realm, the instrument of the emperor's victory in the struggle against the barbarians and the infidels. Thus Géza holds it in his hand as the guarantee of the victory of the Christian ruler. As a result of a peculiar imitation, the same emblem is due to Empress Maria, the imperial couple always being the incarnation of Constantine the Great and St. Helena. It was St. Helena who found the relic and started its cult. Thus Basilissa Maria raises the victorious cross as the "new Helena".

At this point, the Greek crown refers to certain legends related to St. Stephen. Data from authoritative sources prove that Stephen received—set probably in a pectoral cross—a small piece of the True Cross from his wartime ally Basil II of Byzantium. Generally speaking, the cult of the victory-bringing relic can be followed almost uninterruptedly from the time of the very first king throughout Hungarian history. The patriarchal cross of the Hungarian arms, to be dealt with later, also points to the True Cross relic.

Reverting to Géza, we know that Michael Ducas, threatened by his enemies, sought and found an ally in the Hungarian king. The latter's marriage was a preliminary or a confirmation of the alliance. He married a Byzantine noblewoman who belonged to the Synadenos family, and who was a niece of the would-be emperor. The name of the Byzantine princess had emerged earlier already, in connection with the crown (Mrs. Bárány-Oberschall). The observations that can be *42* deduced from the object confirm this view: the *corona graeca* is an emblem shaped in keeping with the prescriptions and traditions of the Byzantine imperial court, and destined to the Hungarian queen coming from Constantinople.

The Western Crown

The upper hemisphere formed by two crossing bands is the most questionable part of the Hungarian crown, and it is the most difficult to treat. According to traditional ideas, it is the remnant of Pope Sylvester's crown. According to more recent suppositions, it is connected with King Stephen in other ways. In Kelleher's attempt at reconstruction it was considered an ornamental part of a book cover, reliquary or portable altar made at Stephen's orders. Recently, György Györffy brought up arguments to support Ödön Polner's earlier theory that the cross-band was the mounting of Stephen's head reliquary, a relic warranting the sacred character of the crown made out of it.

Mrs. Bárány-Oberschall, Boeckler and Deér did not deal with reconstruction; theirs is the merit, however, of having analysed this work of art. Their results differ just as much as the theories aimed at reconstruction.

The object was made the following way. The branches were carefully soldered to the square plaque in the centre by slipping them a few millimetres under it. This was followed by fixing, i.e. soldering, the beaded wire borders, the filigree, then the stone and pearl settings, and the simple settings of the enamels. Finally, the stones, pearls and enamels were placed in their settings. When joining the square central plaque and the branches, great importance was attributed to the alternating rhythm of the stones and pearls. The setting of the upper apostolic plaques was soldered to the beaded wire frame of the central, main plaque; therefore the thinner beaded wire bordering the individual settings was omitted in this instance. The enamels show: in the central square plaque Christ Enthroned, and on the branches, superimposed, two Apostles each in a standing position with their names given in Latin. Obviously, originally all the twelve Apostles were represented. The imprint of the enamels can clearly be seen on the reverse side of the none too thick gold plaque serving as a base. It is evident from this that the pictures of the four missing Apostles were on the lower end of the branches; all that remains of them is a narrow space indicating their place. On the base plaque there are ruptures which are joined with hoops and braided wire. By and large, the cracks follow the horizontal line of the setting of the enamels; obviously, the base split where it resisted bending and pressure the most. A few of the enamels have slipped up within their setting, while the one covered by the Christ plaque has shifted downwards, with its lower portion not following the band's curve. Only two of the plaques presently visible are completely flat. The right corner of the upper one which illustrates St. James has been bent in, and, consequently, the enamel cracked slantwise. The plaque representing St. Peter is bent in the opposite direction as much as the golden streak below the inscription allowed it. These deformities may have two causes: one is a great blow or fall which caused the crown to become dented and the cross at the top to become crooked; the other is the shaping of the bands after the crown was assembled. The decoration of bent surfaces with flat enamels can only be done in case of proper proportions. Here, the enamels are too large for the curves of the branches. Finally, there are no traces on the cross-bands of their having been dismantled from another object; therefore we are probably dealing with some independent object itself, which has retained its original shape except for the fact that the ends of the four branches were cut off.

43

The central enamel
of the Western Crown portrays Christ Enthroned.
Around Him, arranged crosswise in pairs,
are eight Apostles:
SS. Peter and Paul
SS. James and John
SS. Andrew and Philip.
The figure of St. Thomas
is in the most part overlapped by the Ducas plaque,
whereas that of St. Bartholomew is completely
covered by the Byzantine Christ plaque.

SCS PETRVS

SCS ANDREAS

At first glance, this seems to confirm the "skull reliquary" theory. There is, however, one serious difficulty: there never was a human skull on which these bands, together with the plaques, could be fitted; and the real purpose of Byzantine reliquary settings was precisely that, to adorn the relic itself by fitting it closely.

To imagine the original object, we can most certainly start by taking the missing Apostles into account and by adding the filigree frames below. The diameter of the cross with shafts of equal length thus formed will be more than 46 centimetres—a considerable size. The bands were either entirely flat, or were curved very slightly, in an arch much flatter than at present.

On the basis of this, I consider another solution to be more likely; yet, because of the scant documentary material at my disposal, I present my idea as a hypothesis. In the liturgy of the Orthodox Church, an object called "asterisk" is used even today. It is placed over the pieces of Eucharistic bread which have been prepared for consecration and put on the paten; its purpose is to prevent the veil used as a cover from touching the sacrificial food. A single, very modest, Byzantine example of these asterisks is known; it probably dates from the eleventh century and is a relic from Constantinople (Dumbarton Oaks Collection, Washington D.C.). The fact that the object had been used in the Middle Ages is proved by the mosaic in the St. Sophia Church of Kiev depicting the Communion of the Apostles. The asterisks on the relic presently in Washington and in the mosaic at Kiev are unadorned; in addition, the Washington object can be folded to a horseshoe shape along the joining dowel. Among later examples there are adorned asterisks, and their form is varied. The size of the asterisk is determined by the paten or "discus" belonging to it. Not many of these have been left to us either, but there are fine specimens among them, made of alabaster, with cloisonné enamel on a gold base. The best known is the Halberstadt paten (Cathedral Treasury, Halberstadt) of the eleventh century, a gilt silver piece with a diameter of over 40 centimetres. It shows a monumental Crucifixion scene in repoussé; other such objects represent the Pantocrator or The Last Supper or again St. Michael. Earlier examples are adorned with the Communion of the Apostles. The iconography of the chalices and the liturgical veils show that the ensemble of Christ and the Apostles can easily be inserted into this iconographic sphere. At first glance, this concept multiplies the contradictions connected with the cross-band: is it possible that we are faced with an object of Eastern liturgy originating from the sphere of Western art and bearing Latin inscriptions? I shall deal with this problem after outlining the situation from the art historical point of view.

The technique of the enamels was much debated, but the question can now be considered settled. The techniques used on the Christ image in the middle and on the apostle enamels are identical. Their effect, however, is different. In the Pantocrator picture in the typical cloisonné enamel style, the gold base comes into full effect *(Senkschmelz),* while the crowded, decorative composition of the Apostle plaques is actually more closely related to the "full enamel" *(Vollschmelz)* specimens of early Western cloisonné enamel. The similarity of the enamel palette, the details of the cloison designs and the recurring decorative motifs make the unity of the series indisputable. It is all the more peculiar that while the proportions and the posture of the sitting figure are well-balanced and faultless, the standing figures of the Apostles are compressed, and disproportionate. While the craftsman elegantly solved the more difficult task of depicting the figure on the throne, he was apparently at a loss when trying to represent the simpler, standing figures. For instance, on the legs of John and Philip he applied a pleat—a solution reminding the viewer of sitting figures. The placement of the belts on some of the Apostles also corresponds more 54 to the proportions of sitting figures. The scale was apparently determined by the representation of Christ. The heads and the limbs of the Apostles are the same size as His. According to Deér, the irregularities are due to the fact that the models for the Apostles were sitting figures. However, the faultlessly represented sitting figure obviously casts doubt upon the validity of this explanation. This is why Deér, just like other researchers, tried to find the direct analogues of the Apostles.

Let us not reject simple explanations! The figures of the Apostles depicted were dictated by the space available for the whole composition, just as was often the case with figures in the corners of tympanums or with the figure at the edge of the group of prophets on the coronation mantle. After all, the artist had to decorate a prescribed surface, in keeping with an established system, using a given number of protagonists. As for the period and place of the enamels' production, it is most unusual that almost all experts consider Hungary as the likely place, yet views about the period differ widely. In addition to Kelleher, it is primarily Mrs. Bárány-Oberschall who (recently criticizing even Deér's view) consistently looks for the origins of the work among Western cloisonné enamels, specifically in the later phase of Ottonian art. This art had a decisive influence on the workshops in Stephen's court. Deér, however, who suggested the latest date thus far, used the works of the best specialists in the history of the European goldsmith's craft when formulating his own view. According to him, the plaques had been made in Hungary in the first quarter or in the first thirty years of the thirteenth century, but, under the influence of Western, Venetian works, in a Byzantinizing style (mitre of Linköping; enamel adornment of the Bressanone gloves).

The criticism of Hungarian experts was elicited by Deér's method of analysis—a method apparently differing from the classical practice followed in art history. In the absence of actual analogues, however, the indirect approach cannot be objected to *per se;* on the contrary, it is the sole expedient method. Boeckler proceeded in the same way, and it is he who has most pertinently characterized the Western Romanesque style of the pictures so far. He pointed out the marked outlines of the figures of the Apostles, their massiveness, the strictly single-axis structure of their bodies, and also the closed construction of the ornamental fields surrounding the figures. This characterization must be somewhat expanded and clarified, though. In my opinion, the structure of the figures is characterized mostly by articulation, by the clear indication of the waist and, in

some instances, by the stress placed on the legs and their stylized design, whether the figure is sitting or standing. Attire does not play the role of drapery here; it is an ornamental, structural element. When designing John's legs, the master did not hesitate using three different colours in the folds of the cloak, stylizing the disproportionate design of the legs into an abstract ornamental detail. A similar decorative motif can be observed on the Christ plaque where the lower white tunic and its border constitute a peculiar frame at His legs. This conception of the figures and this stylization of the attire are expressly at variance with the drapery figures based on antique traditions and predominant in Byzantine or Byzantinizing cloisonné enamel. This is a characteristic feature of

Romanesque art, with the additional trait that the static figures float rather than stand. The cloak continues behind their legs. Other examples of this rendition can only be found on the earliest relics of Western Romanesque champlevé enamel. A composition similar to the Apostle plaques of the crown can be observed in the same group of relics as far as the relationship between figure and background is concerned. The figures, sometimes rendered without enamel, using the technique of engraving, and sometimes even of a three-dimensional nature, appear in front of an enamelled background of connected tendrils or scattered motifs. The manner in which these enamel compositions are "cut into pieces", often with the patternless streaks of the basic plate, is similar to the plaques on the crown. The ornamental elements, of course, are not and cannot be identical. The master of the cloisonné enamel applied the traditional elements of his own technique. It is typical of champlevé enamel to place several colours beside one another in a delimited field; similar solutions can be observed also in our cloisonné enamels. Another technical peculiarity: sometimes, when shaping the folds of the attire, gold cloisons were applied, with wholly or partially undulating lines. To my knowledge, this occurs only on Western enamels, and never on Byzantine works; it is unknown also in the Venetian group, which is considered as direct antecedent by Deér. In view of the relics known to us, it seems to be a unique element of eleventh-century art. Such traits were the most characteristic features of a given workshop. With the corresponding relics missing, it is impossible to decide whether this is a proof of the masters' conservative outlook or of the survival of the Western tradition. The analogies with the champlevé enamels and also the characteristics of style point to the work having been produced between 1160 and 1180, most probably in the milieu of a court, because gold cloisonné enamel can mainly be found in these places, in addition to Venice, which was exposed to direct Byzantine influence. As the place of production, Hungary may very well be taken into consideration, although the points often referred to as proofs do not decide the issue. One theory, advocated quite long ago, was that the maker of the Christ plaque simply imitated or copied the Pantocrator plaque of the *corona graeca*, which was certainly in Hungary by 1070. In addition, Deér also considered the royal Hungarian seals, made at the beginning of the thirteenth century, as models. He referred to the leg position of the royal figures on the throne as well as to the stylized design of the sun and the moon located on each side of the rulers' heads; these designs replaced the monograms of Christ shown at the sides of the Western Pantocrator. Astral symbols, however, could be observed elsewhere and earlier, too, at the sides of Christ or of an enthroned king. An inverse route of the motif is also probable; it might have been transmitted from the Christ pictures to the sphere of the royal symbols.

The other concordance with the Christ picture of the Greek crown is undoubtedly more significant, since the cypresses at the sides of the enthroned Christ are represented only on these two plaques. However, the rendition and the details of the two figures are so divergent, the "transcription" has succeeded so well, that one cannot talk here about imitation, only about coinciding iconography, adding, at the same time, that there are certain discrepancies here, too, precisely because of the astral symbols.

So far, the enamel colours of the two parts have been dealt with in general terms only. It is worthwhile to present here the two series together and compared to each other. It is generally known that the enamel colour range of the early Middle Ages is more limited than that of later periods; intermediate shades or tints rarely occur. Thus we find on both parts of the crown essentially identical colours, making, however, totally different general impressions and having different characteristics. The colours are: white, yellow, black, brown, red, green, three shades of blue, and flesh colour. All the colours are opaque except the green which is translucent. On the Byzantine crown, the dominant colour is blue—its dark, medium and light varieties; the green occurs in subsidiary details only, while yellow is very frequent, mainly for indicating gold, probably the golden texture and pattern of clothing and attire. The flesh colour of all of the figures is an identical shade; their hair is black, except for the Hungarian king whose hair and beard are brownish. In applying the colours, the Byzantine master always took meticulous care concerning the clarity and sense of design and composition, as well as the traditional forms of representation. *56*

The figures of the saints, represented in pairs, are rendered more varied by a discreet touch; on the secondary details, the colours alternate.

On the upper part, the range of the blue colours begins with a pale, whitish tint, continues with light-blue and reaches a medium-blue shade. The pale tint, in keeping with its role, is a stylized white, i.e. the colour of animals and of old men's hair. For representing the colour of hair, the artist also used brown and black, and as for flesh colour, he used a dark shade and a pale one. In addition, white was used relatively freely, mainly in the rosettes and tendrils of the base. The most essential difference in comparison to the Greek enamels is in the use of translucent green which, together with blue, is the principal colour of the attire here and is sometimes applied on large surfaces, and as background. The goldsmith of the Latin crown used yellow sparingly; a pale shade of it was used on Christ's throne only. The Western master's stylized and decorative colour treatment has already been dealt with, as was his tendency to apply colours next to each other, without cloisons. No doubt he did so consciously. On one point the technique seems less perfect than that of Byzantine enamels: in one or two places, the colours flow over from the cloisons.

Very few relics of Romanesque cloisonné enamel are known, and most of them are merely ornamental. Therefore, within their own genre, the analogous plaques probably never can be placed beside each other. However, the filigree frame of gems and pearls does have an analogy, viz. the two plaques of the head reliquary crown of St. Oswald, preserved in the Hildesheim Cathedral. The trapezoidal plaques used in that reliquary are, in all probability, the remnants of an *armilla* or bracelet worn on the upper arm. Their dates of origin, not indicated by the ornamental enamel decoration of the two plaques, must be close to that of the crown-band, i.e. between A.D. 1000 and 1300. The filigree frames consist of heart-shaped palmettes decorated with regular stones between the pearls, ground into drop shapes on the crown and into oval shapes on the Hildesheim enamels. Apart from the stones and the pearls, the affinity of the Hungarian sceptre and with the fragments found in the royal tombs at Székesfehérvár is undeniable. Historical evidence shows that the finds originate from the twelfth century and not earlier. As we have seen, the features of the enamels on the *corona latina* point to the same period. On the other hand, the heart-shaped palmette filigree is of Byzantine origin; the nearest Byzantine analogy to the stone filigree, a gold pectoral cross with regular droplike and round stones (British Museum, London), is again dated from the twelfth century.

If reconstruction involving the "asterisk" stands the test of further examination, it could become a most important argument in favour of the object originating in Hungary. In the given period, it was precisely Hungary where the making of an object Western in character but belonging to Eastern liturgy was highly conceivable. Here again we must refer mainly to Moravcsik's classic works. From the beginnings of missionary activity up to the end of the thirteenth century, there were Byzantine religious institutions in Hungary which could operate undisturbed even after the Schism. The best known was the Greek nunnery of Veszprémvölgy founded by St. Stephen, probably at the time of the arrival in Hungary of his future daughter-in-law, a Byzantine princess. Andrew I, who had been baptized in Kiev and married a Russian princess, founded new Orthodox institutions. Even a papal letter of 1204 talks about many Greek Orthodox monasteries in Hungary; their names, however, have mostly been lost and only a few are known to us. Let us not forget that, several times, Byzantium gave queens to the royal court of Hungary. If Orthodox monasteries could function, it is also conceivable that there was, in the royal court, an Orthodox priest in the queen's service. Very few relics of Eastern-rite liturgy and of the activities of Byzantine priests have survived. St. Stephen's purse (Treasury, Vienna) and a twelfth-century embroidered reliquary with Old Slavonic liturgical inscriptions and Byzantine-type illustrations are worth mentioning in this context.

Nothing has been said so far about the simple cross adorning the summit of the crown. I shall deal with this later when speaking about the assembly of the two crowns.

The Coronation Mantle: King Stephen's and Queen Gisela's Chasuble

The coronation mantle is the sole item that has survived from among the coronation vestments. The most authentic source informing us about its origins is its embroidered inscription: ANNO INCARNACIONIS XPI: M: XXXI: INDICCIONE: XIIII A STEPHANO REGE ET GISLA REGINA CASVLA HEC OPERATA ≁(est) ET DATA ECCLESIAE SANCTA(e) MARIAE SITAE IN CIVITATE ALBA, i.e. "this chasuble was ordered to be made and given to the Church of St. Mary situated in the city of Alba by King Stephen and Queen Gisela in the 1031st year of Christ's incarnation, in the 14th indiction". The Church of St. Mary was the king's private church, and Székesfehérvár the Aachen (Aix-la-Chapelle) of Hungary, while the provostal church was the burial-place of its founder and several of his successors, as well as the coronation church of the Hungarian kings. King Stephen generously furnished it with ecclesiastical vestments. One of these is the splendid chasuble—perhaps the most beautiful of all early medieval embroidered textiles.

The basic material of the chasuble, which is almost completely covered by embroidery work of golden and silk thread, is a faded and deteriorated silk fabric *(samitum),* with an endless pattern of green and purple rosettes. Gold predominates in the embroidery, while the second most common colour is indigo-blue, beautiful and vivid even today. The green, which was once dominant, has now, however, faded into a yellowish tobacco-colour. The golden thread was arranged across the surface and was stitched down mostly with red silk thread. In some places, though, this stitching was in brownish and uncoloured silk thread *(Anlegetechnik).* The contours were embroidered with red silk, and the detail in the gold patches with a variety of colours. Only six varieties of stitching were used. The framework of the composition is the usual adornment of the ample bell-shaped, medieval chasubles, "the fork cross". The streaks dividing the surface and the mandorlas around each design are joined to this, populating the composition with a multitude of figures of varied size and designed in different ways. Some of the figures have their names embroidered next to them, and the scenes framed by mandorlas are supplied with explanatory texts.

The ensemble consists mostly of traditional images each of which has a definite meaning. The composition as a whole, however, expressed a specific and unique message at the time. Every attempt at interpretation has tried to reconstruct this particular message. János Horváth saw the unit as a *Credo* illustration; and, more recently, Endre Tóth as the visualization of the All-Saints' litany. Contemporary analogies, such as the textile works made in the court of German Emperor Henry II, Stephen's brother-in-law (the so-called "mantle of Kunigunda" and the "Star" mantle in Bamberg Cathedral), point to the view according to which the pictures and the inscriptions have to be interpreted as elements of identical value, a vocabulary, as it were, of a peculiar procedure of illustration. The inscriptions on the mantle belong to the genre of the so-called *tituli* (captions);

such *tituli* commented mainly monumental representations and mostly in versified form. There are Leonine hexameters on Stephen's chasuble. The pictures and the inscriptions together represent one of the most popular Christian hymns, the thanksgiving song beginning with the words *Te Deum.* The text of the hymn, attributed to St. Ambrose, dates probably from the fifth century and was composed of various texts. The same celestial choirs which, according to the hymn, glorify God together, appear on the chasuble. They are not actual groups, but the individual parts of the structure required by the composition. The term "All the Angels" of the text refers, for example, to the half-length portraits arranged on the branch of the fork cross and to the angels holding the oval frames placed on the shoulder. The enumeration, in the hymn, of the choirs singing the glory of God differs in one point from the list of the images on the mantle. Below the angels, in the two segments beneath the shoulders, all the major and minor Old Testament prophets, altogether sixteen, can be seen. The standing figures become smaller and smaller as they proceed towards the sides; this is due to the limited space available, but, at the same time, it indicates the prophets' rank and status, the four great prophets occupying a place of honour at the sides of Christ appearing in the centre of both groups. The exalted apostolic body sits enthroned underneath ornate arcades, in the full glory of heavenly Jerusalem. Some of the Apostles—not only the Evangelists appear as writers, depicted with pens and other writing utensils. Below the circular row of Apostles on the chasuble, in the lowest band, there are three-quarter-length figures framed with medallions; these are the first martyrs of the Church referred to in the Mass, or, to quote the text of the hymn, the splendid army of martyrs.

The figures, placed in separate frames, together with their inscriptions, illustrate the other part of the hymn, i.e. the various expressions used to glorify Christ, the king of glory, who was born to save the world, who conquered death and who will come again to hold judgement. The Christ victorious over death is the one in the middle of the back section, standing and treading on the asp and the basilisk; whereas the Christ who sits on God's right and indicates the Last Judgement is the enthroned figure beneath the former one, inserted into the row of Apostles. This is clearly expressed by both the traditional images and by the inscriptions. The correct interpretation of the two smaller mandorlas on the shoulder was aided by the unstitching of folds, thereby enabling the exact design of all the details to be ascertained. Formerly, the two small pictures beneath the collar could not be seen clearly. These benedictory *manus Dei* pictures also indicate the lateral axis of the one-time chasuble, and undoubtedly are related to the figures shown below them. A left hand raised in blessing and depicted in a square-framed aureole appertains to the picture of Mary lifting her arms in an early attitude of prayer. This is to be found on the left shoulder. The corresponding right hand with nimbus on the right-hand side is of greater importance. The earlier interpretation of the figure on the right, surrounded in the circlet by beams light, must therefore be modified. Despite the chalice (ornamental vessel) situated at its feet, this figure cannot be St. John the Evangelist. It must be, in keeping with the inscription, the supreme king *(summus rex)* or, to use another term, the Pantocrator—often associated, in other compositions as well—with the "godly parent". The scene is the heavenly sphere—and this interpretation is confirmed by the inscriptions, the angels and the picture of the four living creatures.

The singers of the hymn finally invoke Jesus; they request Him to help His servants whom He had saved at the price of His precious blood. "Sign of the cross, certain hope of salvation", reads the Latin inscription at the border of the once square-framed design at the neck of the chasuble—a design which almost completely fell victim to alterations, probably together with

The inscriptions on the Coronation Mantle:
Victorious Christ: HOSTIBVS EN XPISTVS PROSTRATIS EMICAT ALT(us)+
Enthroned Christ: SESSIO REGNANTEM NOTAS ET XPM DOMINANTEM
Mary (on left shoulder): EMICAT IN CELO SANCTAE GENITRICIS IMAGO
Christ (on right shoulder): DAT SVMMO REGI FAMVLATVM CONCIO CELI
Fragment of the cross, on the breast: SIGNVM CRVCIS O SPES CERTA SALVT(is)
Fragment of picture, on the breast: RRET OBVMBRA

the word ECCE, to serve in all likelihood, as the beginning of the inscription. References were made earlier to the two remaining extremities of the arm of the cross. Today, however, we know for certain that not only the cross was visible but also the crucified Christ; His hand can be clearly recognized. In addition, beneath the transverse beam of the Cross, we can obviously expect to find the figures of Mary and St. John the Evangelist. So not only the cross bringing salvation was depicted—as indicated by the inscription—but also Christ the Saviour to whom the singers' supplication soared. The donors who gave the chasuble to the Church were not only named in the inscription, they are shown among the martyrs, with the queen holding the model of the church on the left, the king wearing royal attire and insignia on the right. In no other place does such an arrangement occur, and it can only be understood with the aid of the hymn: the royal donors are the singers who, at the end of the hymn, beg Christ and His saints to let them share in eternal glory. Moreover, the saints are depicted in a way different from the usual. They have the same royal attire, the same lily-adorned diadem, the same orb and even the same lance as the king. It has been proved recently, on the basis of the coins found at Nagyharsány, that the lance had actually been part of King Stephen's insignia. This phenomenon indicates the same manner of representation (word-illustration) as that of the donors placed among the saints. This method was mainly applied in the illustrations of psalm books, expressing in images even the most peculiar details of the texts. Thus one cannot agree with Györffy in whose opinion the royal couple's "martyrdom"—due to the death of their only son, Emeric—placed them among the saints. This way of thinking is entirely alien to medieval religious conviction according to which the Christian faith delivers man from the valley of tears and leads him to the vision of God.

With all this, the rich gallery of the chasuble has not yet been exhausted. What remains to be done is to decipher the one-time—now incomplete—mandorla, the remnants of which can be seen at the border on the right-hand side. In the course of research, it has been proved that we have to think in terms of a very big picture, i.e. with one that is identical in size with the mandorla on the back, which surrounds the triumphant Christ. This picture area contains, however, not just a single large figure but a whole scene. Of the many interpretations of this which have so far been put forward including my own, the Transfiguration of Jesus (Czobor) seems the most convincing. The main reason here is precisely the size of the picture. This composition is "multi-storeyed", and the protagonists are often not to scale. Accordingly, the upper figure in the incomplete picture is Moses or Elijah, and the smaller, bowed figure below is one of the three disciples. In the stories from the Gospels, the revelation is surrounded by clouds, and the word "overshadows" [obumbra(t)] also occurs as part of the fragmentary inscription on the mandorla. It is highly probable that the wonderful series of pictures depicting Christ seven times and in different ways began precisely with this scene—the revelation of Christ as The Son of God.

The spaces between the towers rising above the arcades of heavenly Jerusalem are populated with small, animated figures—quite different from those of the other protagonists depicted in a grandiose way, in nicely pleated attire. Some time ago, they were considered fighters; this is why I thought that they referred to the symbolic struggle of Good and Evil in the human soul. Györffy recently surmised that the small figures represented the destroyers and the rebuilders of the church in earthly Jerusalem, demolished by Caliph Hakim. Probably none of the explanations is correct. Indeed, there are among the figures armed ones, handling lances, swords or clubs and sometimes in a grouping indicating single combat. Occasionally "snake-charmers" in cross-legged sitting position appear, as do facing figures of "noblemen" in long robes, others lying flat or kneeling and

65

another sitting cross-legged in the posture of a "judge", and even a group of "pilgrims" holding small crosses as they move on. Maria-Madeleine Gauthier pointed out that they are *outside* the paradisiacal sphere of the enthroned Christ and the group of Apostles; therefore the little figures may be the representatives of "the peoples of the Earth", and the hymn, "Deliver, O Lord, Your people", is sounded for their sake as well. Their role may be similar also to that of the fantastic carved decorations in the churches. The reconstruction of the original chasuble is also a task to be solved, as is the clarification of the principles determining the decorative system of the conical form. Inferences as to the relative size of the part cut out of the front can be made on the basis of the composition and of the incomplete designs. A not very wide streak, narrowing upwards, was cut out to form the semicircular mantle. The neckline of bell-shaped chasubles is generally a hole or a somewhat widened slash at most. Earlier I thought that the clasp used to fasten the present mantle, together with the piece used as a patch in the left front section over the outermost prophet figure, was originally the border of the neckline. As a matter of fact, there exists a third fragment: another patch, on the bottom edge of the other wing, on St. Lawrence's breast. The objects, which were originally continuous, are decorated with half-length portraits in medallions. Their style, including the golden embroidery fixed with red, resembles that of the chasuble. The difference is that the spaces are densely covered with golden embroidery so that the material serving as the base is not visible. Under the microscope, the base material appears to be of a single shade of red. Therefore, the question as to whether the series of medallions was cut off from the mantle remains unanswered for the time being. Should this be the case, i.e. if they really had been cut off, two things are most probable. Firstly, both the scale and the pure gold indicate the lower border, and secondly, the chasuble was spoiled when it was turned into a mantle.

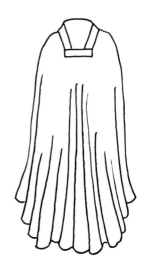

Between the figures of the royal couple, on the vertical shaft of the fork cross, there is again the half-length portrait of an unidentified youth. For a long time it has been thought to represent Prince Emeric, and it is indeed difficult to conceive any other interpretation. Earlier it was even thought that the chasuble had been made at the time of the death of the prince. However, there were two of the anonymous young men. The border of the medallion and the top of the lower figure's head have been left, the rest was cut away. The anonymous secular figures might be the deceased children of the donating couple. However, the modest way in which they are shown hardly points to the donation of the chasuble. It is much more likely that part of the church at Fehérvár was consecrated in 1031, perhaps on 15 August. This was the Feast of the Assumption, the Day of Our Lady, to whom the church had been dedicated. Legend has it that King Stephen wished to die on this feast day, and did in fact do so. The possible first consecration of the royal church on its name-giving day might have been an appropriate occasion for the donation of a chasuble of a laudatory tone and royal sumptuousness.

In any case, fixing the year at 1031 is sufficient to contradict the theory that the work had been ordered from a German workshop, as the war that had been started by Conrad II's aggression had hardly ended by this time. The missionary king, organizer of the Church, who, in his legislation, undertook the obligation to furnish the churches, could not possibly do without craftsmen. What is more, there were surely workshops in this period which could look back on some past activity. Some of the craftsmen might have come to Hungary with the suite of Gisela, Princess of Bavaria, or might have settled in this country somewhat later, from places connected with the family such as the lands of German Emperor Henry II, Gisela's elder brother. Queen Gisela, just as Henry II's wife, is depicted as one of the benefactors on the chasuble. Together with Stephen, Queen Gisela,

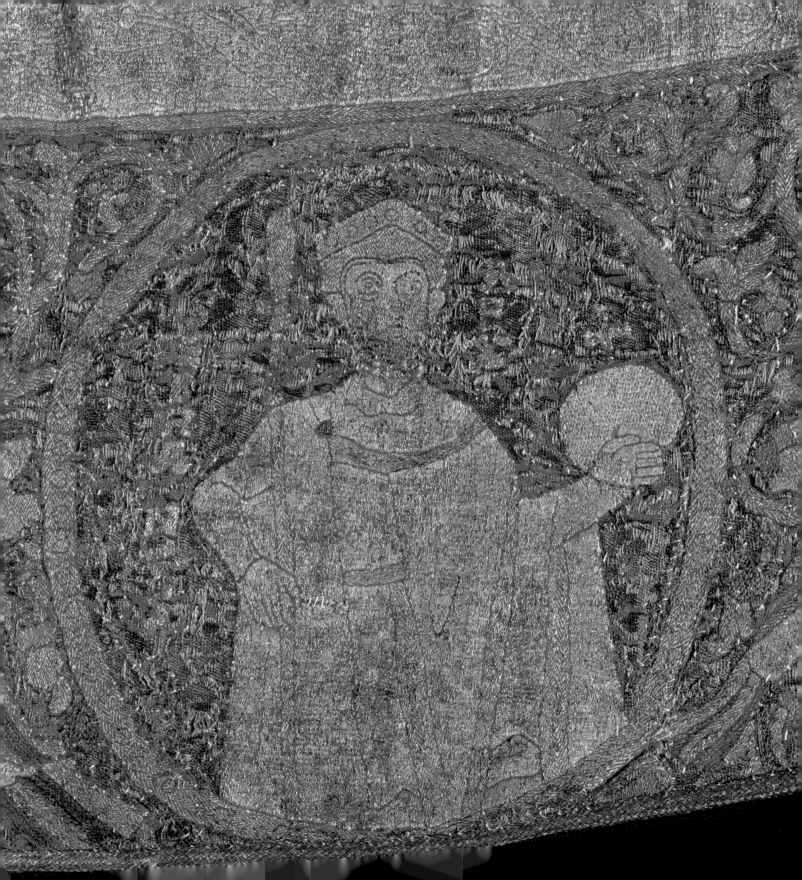

his "beloved wife" *(dilecta sibi coniunx),* is the co-donor of the embroidered chasuble sent by the royal couple to the Pope, "The Apostolic Lord John", and which at one time was kept at Metz.

According to legend and tradition, the pious queen herself participated in the making of gifts to the Church. This tradition is usually mentioned in connection with the activity of the Byzantine nunnery in Veszprémvölgy, a valley near Veszprém in Western Hungary, where, it is said, the nuns and the lay canonesses of the royal court worked together. Such a possibility cannot be excluded; however, the study of the chasuble increasingly suggests that in this case we are dealing with a complicated craft requiring training. As to the working conditions of the craftsmen and the process by which similar works were made, there are, alas, only conjectures. Undoubtedly, however, the composition of the great pictorial ensemble of the chasuble and the beautifully formulated Latin inscriptions must be attributed to a cleric of high ecclesiastical and literary erudition—probably a priest in the royal court.

The technique of the embroidery is of Byzantine origin, and numerous Byzantine features can be pointed out in the style of the embroidery on the chasuble. This influence, however, came to Hungary, together with the Carolingian tradition, through the intermediary of the art of the German imperial court. German researchers generally think that the chasuble was actually made there, at the favourite residence of Gisela's family, Ratisbon (Regensburg), together with the related relics produced at the commission of Emperor Henry II and his wife. A limited relationship can be shown, indeed, although mainly in connection with miniatures. The grandiose composition of the chasuble expressly differs from the style of the Ratisbon textiles. The analogies of a number of its details, and of the whole as well, can be found in works grouped not so much around Ratisbon but rather Reichenau, and not so much in textiles as in goldsmith's works. The analogy of Christ's great standing figure can be seen in the centre of the Basle gold altar frontal made at Emperor Henry II's commission (Musée de Cluny, Paris), and that of the space-filling decoration consisting of pairs of birds and scroll-work on the cover of an evangeliary (Bayerische Staatsbibliothek, Munich). Quite a number of such analogies could be listed. The turreted arcades of the row of Apostles occur in the form which characterizes bone carving, with special importance attributed to rich details. In the last analysis, the composition of the chasuble, divided into well-defined parts, is also related to the structure of great goldsmith's works, mainly of altar frontals. The monumental figures embroidered in gold—and suggesting some plasticity—also remind the experts of these works. (It is, by the way, probable that in order to obtain a uniform and brilliant surface effect, the golden embroidery was planished.)

The German analogies are, generally speaking, of an earlier date than the chasuble made in 1031. The group of small, animated figures points, on the other hand, to the beginning of a later stylistical trait. This "mixture" is a local speciality—a typical feature of the royal Hungarian workshop originating from the initiatives at the beginning of the eleventh century. The large gold reliquary cross preserved in Munich (Schatzkammer der Residenz), a gift of Stephen's wife for the tomb of her mother, Gisela of Burgundy (d. 1006), is of a similar style. The cross might have been made at the time the chasuble was produced. An interesting fact: while the composition of the chasuble suggests goldsmith's works to have been its model, the unique frame of the cross, consisting of enamel plaques and pearls, is reminiscent of the border on Byzantine gala robes. Most probably, goldsmiths and textile artists collaborated closely—a fact again pointing to Hungary as the country of origin.

The chasuble transformed into a mantle was held in high esteem. When the thin silk covered

with heavy embroidery became extensively damaged, the entire mantle was transferred to a new base, while preserving the split remnants of the old fabric. This happened probably in 1608, on the orders of Matthias II. This was a procedure of rare efficacy. The Bamberg relics, for example, were also restored in the sixteenth century, but there the base material was simply removed and the remaining pieces of embroidery were sewn on again in a somewhat haphazard order. Today, the mantle is entirely covered with repair-stitches; in spite of this, the overall picture is quite clear, the large details being almost entirely intact. The mantle was exposed to random stitching for centuries, for it became a tradition that before coronations the queen and her ladies-in-waiting mended it. Modern restorers are justifiably horrified at this; and yet, this procedure helped the eight-and-a-half-century-old chasuble to survive the vicissitudes to which it was exposed.

The style of the mantle's collar differs from that of the chasuble, and the technique used represents the other variation of gold embroidery in which the stiffly stitched-down gold thread is embedded into the basic material *(versenkte Anlegetechnik)*. And also, it was attached to the opened chasuble in an inverse position. Judging by its bordered composition, it must have been an independent piece. On a pale red, faded base, there is an arcaded decoration, with a scroll ornament embroidered with gold and stylized pairs of animals, griffins, peacocks, squirrels in between. The pale, faded bluish-green contour can still be seen in some places. It is covered with a large number of tiny pearls; decorative motifs of filigree-like thin golden braid are attached to the embroidery, reminiscent of the filigreed setting of the sceptre. This concordance, as well as the braid motifs, frequently applied in Byzantine embroidery (reliquary purse, Germanisches Nationalmuseum, Nuremberg), indicate that the object was obviously made in a workshop having direct Byzantine connections, probably in Béla III's court workshop in the third quarter of the twelfth century.

It is interesting that the object most closely related to it is the so-called "St. Stephen's cap" (Treasury, Vienna) which used to be associated with the coronation mantle. The relationship is also indicated by the abstract decorative elements appearing together with the fine animal and tendril motifs and by the identical structure of the composition. St. Stephen's cap was made of an embroidered fragment from another garment, perhaps from the lower border of a gala dress.

As far as the original purpose of the collar is concerned, one must return to Arnold Ipolyi's definition of the beautiful embroidery as *amictus parura*. This was the ornate upper border of the amice (or neckerchief) worn even today by the priest between his alb and chasuble. As shown by innumerable illustrations, it was worn above the chasuble as a big, upright shoulder-collar, completing the chasuble as it were.

The Closed Crown and the Coronation Mantle

The present form of the mantle and the crown came about as a result of identical procedures, viz. various finished objects were assembled, with minor alterations. In the process no attempt was made to avoid damaging such venerable pictures as the crucified Christ on the chest of the chasuble or the Latin Pantocrator at the peak of the crown whose picture was cruelly pierced by the dowel of the cross. Making these alterations must have been a fairly simple job indeed. It is almost certain that the two regalia were produced at the same time and for the same occasion. According to Deér, they were prepared in a haste, particularly as far as the crown was concerned. As a matter of fact, one cannot speak of "expert" procedure in this instance; it should not be forgotten, however, that

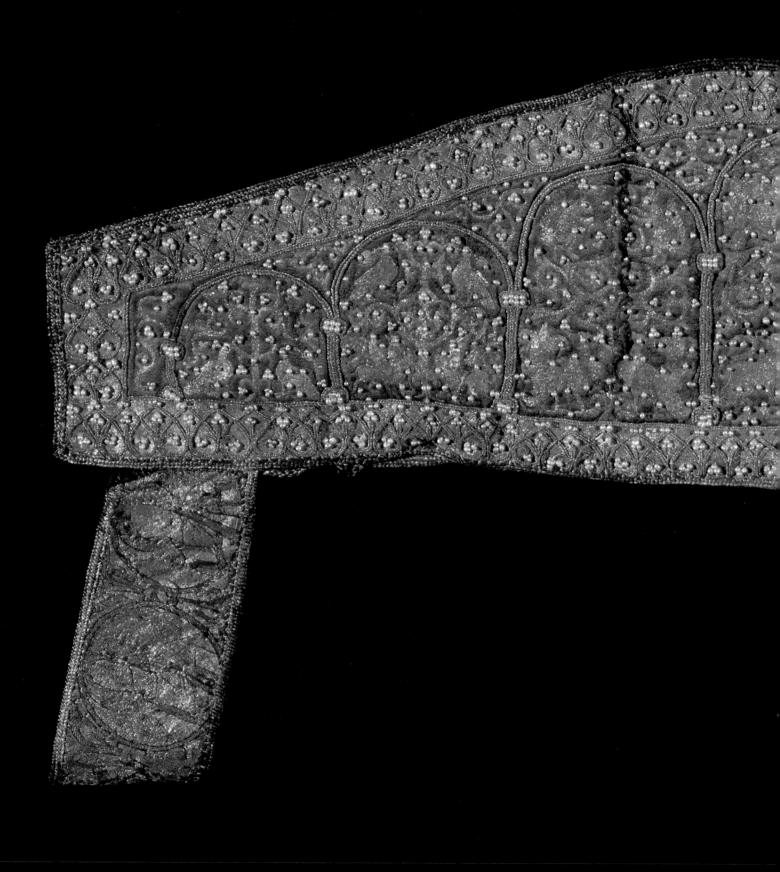

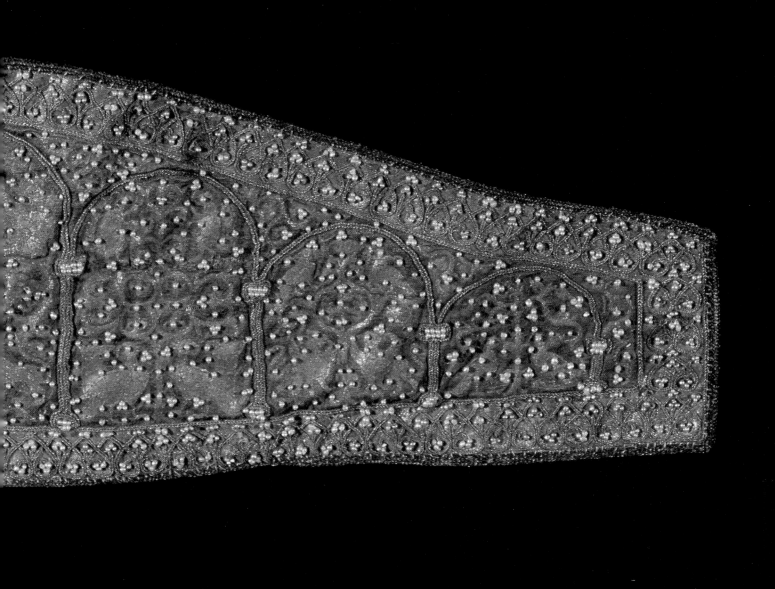

in the Middle Ages such amateurish alteration and repair of even the most carefully guarded items was common, and not necessarily an indication of haste.

The chasuble was no doubt kept in the treasury of the basilica at Székesfehérvár, and so were probably the other component parts too. It is a fact that the safeguarding of the Hungarian coronation insignia was the task of the Székesfehérvár chapter. At the same time, the treasury could have also been the place of preservation for such secular treasures as robes of state, and even of the Byzantine diadem. Medieval rulers often bestowed their jewels, and even their insignia, on the Church. Of the many Hungarian and foreign examples mention should be made of Queen Gisela's whose crown was guarded at Veszprém and was borrowed by Hungarian King Andrew II when he prepared for a crusade.

The most characteristic appurtenance of the new mantle is the collar. The earlier, traditional form of the royal mantle was the semicircular *paludamentum* or *chlamys* of antique origin which was worn fastened on the chest or the shoulder (see King Stephen on the chasuble, or King Géza I on the crown). In whatever fashion it was worn, it had no collar up to the end of the twelfth century. The mantle with a large, flowing collar was the most typical article of clothing worn internationally by knights in the thirteenth century. It was worn quite open and thrown over the shoulder; this is why it was loosely laced with a long clamp or braid. This form first appeared on Andrew II's seal. The *tassieux,* a pair of large jewels sewn on the shoulders, were a characteristic ornament of this garment. This fashion was so widespread in Hungary that the only remaining shoulder ornaments, three pairs, are now preserved in this country (Hungarian National Museum and Museum of Applied Arts, Budapest). We also know that King Stephen V purchased such jewels. With this in mind, the coronation mantle could not have acquired its present form before the thirteenth century. The fact that the cap resembling a child's bonnet, such as the above-mentioned St. Stephen relic in Vienna, which was a fashionable article among the aristocracy of the period, supplies ample food for thought. The thin cap protected the hairdo, and the actual headgear or helmet was worn over it.

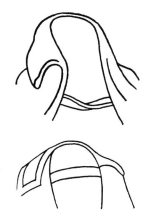

The Vienna cap and purse landed in the treasury coming from the Capuchins to whom it had been donated, so tradition holds, by King Matthias II and his wife; by the same Matthias II who tried to obtain the coronation mantle and the Corvinus Calvary (now in Esztergom) under the pretext of wanting to have them copied. In all probability, the two St. Stephen relics also reached Vienna from Hungary where the holy king's name had become attached to them. What is more, the source of its derivation from Stephen is the same as in the case of the coronation insignia. It is even conceivable that the cap was an accessory of the coronation ensemble, whose components

78

changed and decreased in number in the course of time, and that it had been produced simultaneously with the collared mantle.

Thus, the characteristic form of the mantle may assist, to a certain extent, in deciding the question of when the crown was assembled from the two objects. Earlier, together with the majority of researchers, I was inclined to favour the period of Béla III's reign. The purpose of making a closed crown would have been to imitate the Byzantine emperor's mitre-like emblem of a similar shape, the *kamelaukion*. Precisely during the reign of the Comnenus emperors, the *kamelaukion* acquired great significance in Byzantine protocol. A number of arguments were put forward in support of this theory; in addition to an intention to imitate, the given historical situation was used as explanation. After Manuel's death, King Béla III had a chance to occupy the Byzantine throne for which he had been educated in his childhood. Accordingly, the crown was not merely an imitation, but rather it would actually have been the Byzantine imperial crown made for the occasion in Hungary (Bogyay, Vajay).

Other hypotheses date the transformation of the crown much later, or much earlier. As we have seen, Deér proposed that the crown was transformed on the order of King Stephen V, who was forced to do this because, after their father's death, Princess Anne had the earlier insignia taken out of the country. The new form was created by imitating the old crown which the Byzantine prelate had mentioned in 1166 as a jewel most desirable to possess and which had been called "sacred crown" by 1256. On account of these data, informing as they do about a revered and highly important emblem, Györffy rejected the theory of an imitation crown. Since it is well-known that soon after Stephen I's death his crown had been transferred to Rome, Györffy tried to find out when it had been made and why it was termed "sacred". Györffy considers King Coloman to have been the first owner of the present-day crown. In his view Coloman completed his father's, Géza's, emblem of Byzantine origin with a setting removed from a head-reliquary of the first Hungarian king canonized not long before, modelling the new crown after the crown of the Comnenus dynasty. Apart from the fact that the style of the objects, especially that of the upper part, makes such an early date of the alteration impossible, Györffy's theory is also untenable as far as the relics themselves are concerned. The relics were distributed, and sometimes even sold or pilfered. But to deprive the holy predecessor's relic of the ornaments with which it had recently been adorned in order to put it on one's own head would be a most peculiar manifestation of respect for the saint, especially from a king well versed in ecclesiastical affairs and educated for a clerical career! There are examples for the opposite process only, namely that of rulers granting their own insignia for decorating relics. *Such* examples are quite numerous indeed.

It is to the point, however, to examine the reasons for the "sacred character" of the holy crown. The theory based on the actual form of the crown (closed crown with curved bands) has not proved to be useful, the less so as this form was fairly widespread. Not only Byzantine emperors and Balkan kings had recourse to it; in Western Europe, the Hohenstaufen rulers adopted this form parallel with the Comnenus emperors in the East. In addition to the Byzantine antecedents, it has earlier Western antecedents also. What is more, it was traditional in the close vicinity of Hungary, in Bohemia; the crown of the Přemysl kings was of the same shape in the twelfth century, and later Charles IV used this form also.

It is not the truncated cross-band that is important on the Hungarian crown, but the cross. Christ's image was pierced through because of it, and the bands were mounted precisely so that they provide a place of distinction for the cross, not for the simple cross of today, but for its

The crown from the inside.
Originally the portraits of the now missing four Apostles
were placed at
the ends of the cross-bands.

predecessor. An excellent heraldist, Szabolcs Vajay, called to my attention a strange incident in the crown's history which had completely escaped everybody's attention. Before Queen Isabella handed over the regalia to Ferdinand in 1551, she broke the cross off the crown's peak for her son, John Sigismund. According to a contemporary Polish chronicler, John Sigismund wore this cross on his chest till the end of his life, "...because he who possesses this cross will again come into possession of the missing parts which, *subjected to the power of the cross,* had belonged to it". Later, the cross became the property of Sigismund Báthory who, persuaded by his confessor, bestowed it on Emperor Rudolf II. This was reported by an Italian envoy in Prague who also told the Isabella-John Sigismund story. According to him, the cross was "a lily or something like it, a part and adornment of Hungary's crown". Thus the present cross on the crown is a replacement made after 1551.

Originally, the cross in question was probably not a simple ornament but a reliquary cross. Judging from its ornamental "lily-shaped" setting, it was probably the holder of a fragment from the True Cross, which was usually worn on the chest. The reinforcement of weapons and royal insignia with dominical relics, with the revered remain of the instruments of the Passion, was a long-standing tradition closely bound up with Constantine the Great. It is one of the manifestations of the cult in which the sign of the cross, and later, the veneration of the True Cross, was connected with the Christian ruler's person. As mentioned previously, in the Byzantine emperor's opinion, the Hungarian king deserved a cross-sceptre. Research has proved that veneration of the True Cross dates from St. Stephen's era and that it was by no means an isolated phenomenon. Not only the Byzantine emperors but also Western rulers considered the relic as a "weapon in battle" ensuring victory. It is a special Hungarian feature, however, that the veneration of the True Cross was closely interwoven with the cult of the country's first king.

The most varied elements testify to the veneration of the relic. Its transformation into arms is undoubtedly the most interesting turning-point in this context. This was probably done by Béla III although his sons refrained from making use of it. Starting with Béla IV, the patriarchal cross, the image of the relic, can be traced on the royal seals and even on the seals of the queen. Probably on French influence, the crown of thorns made its appearance together with the cross on the seals of Stephen V. "Crown and cross should warrant this seal's force" reads the exergue on one of the seals.

Several small fragments of the True Cross were in possession of the Árpád dynasty. As a point of interest, it is precisely the smallest ones, those set into the cross on the chest, that are attributed to St. Stephen. About a tiny fragment of the True Cross, a Russian chronicler recording King Géza II's campaigns wrote that it had been the holy king's property and, despite its small size, it was a relic of great force. We are, perhaps, not off the track when surmising that the Hungarian crown was holy because it had once been reinforced with a fragment of the victory-bringing relic. This is also how it comes to be regarded as "St. Stephen's crown"—either because it was adorned with a reliquary cross attributed to the king or because of a relic associated with the holy king's person. If the force of the arms was warranted by relics, why not do the same with the crown? The example of the arms is unique, but we know about quite a few reliquary crowns. To mention but the most obvious example, let us cite Charles IV's crown provided with a cross containing a thorn relic.

The cult of the relic and of the first king is continuous. It would be a futile attempt, for the time being, to try to link the transformation of the crown to this or that phase of the cult, or to pick out one or the other thirteenth-century king as the one on whose orders the closed crown was made. It could have been Andrew II preparing for participation in the Crusades, or the much-tried Béla IV who felt special veneration for the True Cross, or Stephen V who possessed no insignia and in whose favour Deér lists historical arguments worth considering and to whom the new version of the seal must be attributed anyway.

The insignia are means called upon to express ideas, but they are, of course, not identical with the thoughts they express. Were this not the case, it could have never been proposed (after the loss of the original emblems) that the royal insignia of Hungary once belonged to St. Stephen.

The Sceptre

The club-like shape of the Hungarian sceptre, calling to mind a weapon, is unique in medieval Europe. Its antecedents can be found in ancient Oriental cultures; Persian and Sassanid kings were frequently represented with similar insignia of power, insignia provided with a short handle and a globular end. The nomadic cultures of the South Russian steppes drew a great deal from the Sassanid art of Iran, and the club-headed sceptre was also taken over from there. Also in the area of Hungary, pierced bone spheres were found in Avar graves dating from the time of the Great Migrations, spheres provided with a handle, and which no doubt were insignia of rank. At Tagancha, in the Kiev region, a club-shaped silver sceptre with a spherical end had been buried in the grave of a nomadic prince; presumably, the grave was one belonging to those fragmentary groups of Hungarians who had remained in the East. But the art of the Hungarians who settled in the Carpathian Basin is also strongly interspersed with Sassanid influences, so that the *kulturkreis* where this club-shaped emblem of power was used, was by no means alien to them.

The head of the Hungarian sceptre is a pierced rock crystal sphere 7 cm in diameter, with three lions cut into its side. The beasts are represented squatting on their hind legs, with their upturned tails ending in a plant motif, a half palmette. Judged by its marks of style, the crystal sphere is of Islamic origin; according to traditional theory, it was made either in Egypt during the reign of the Fatimid dynasty or in the territory of the Arab caliphate in Iraq, in the tenth century. The art of both areas was strongly influenced by Iranian-Persian traditions, and, in addition to the style of carving, this relationship is also indicated by the purpose of the object, viz. the crystal sphere might have been designed to figure as a sceptre-head.

The Arabs were masters of the difficult technique of crystal carving, and their works enjoyed high esteem in Europe. We have written documents that German Emperor Henry II, St. Stephen's brother-in-law, as well as others, liked and collected rock crystal objects; the head of the sceptre might have come to Hungary from his court. But it could have arrived through direct commercial contacts with the Arabs which are supported by written sources and *dirhems* found in Hungary.

The head of the sceptre is flanked by flower-shaped gold plates above and below, which are held together by three double bands. There is a magic knot made up of an endlessly twisted plaitwork in the centre of the upper, ten-leafed rosette. This was a motif of Oriental origin but widespread throughout Europe and was, in general, a design used to stave off evil. The entire setting of the sceptre-head was covered with an extraordinarily fine and rich filigree pattern. Tiny gold spheres on short little chains hang from the edges of the rosettes; according to medieval belief, their jingle kept away evil spirits. The handle of the sceptre is wooden, with a gilded silver overlay, and with filigree ornament much simpler and coarser than that of the head setting.

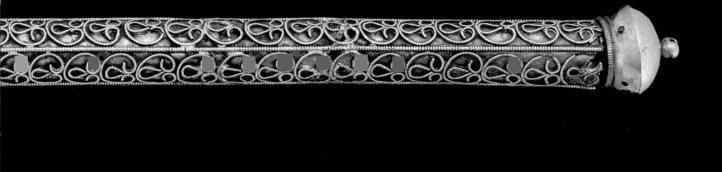

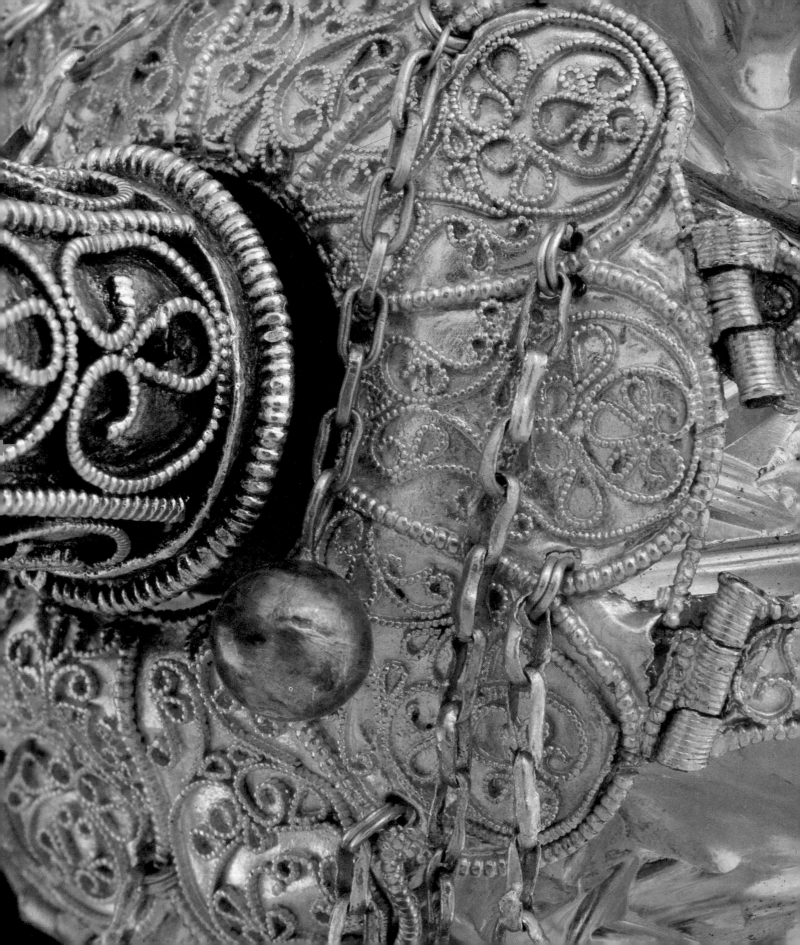

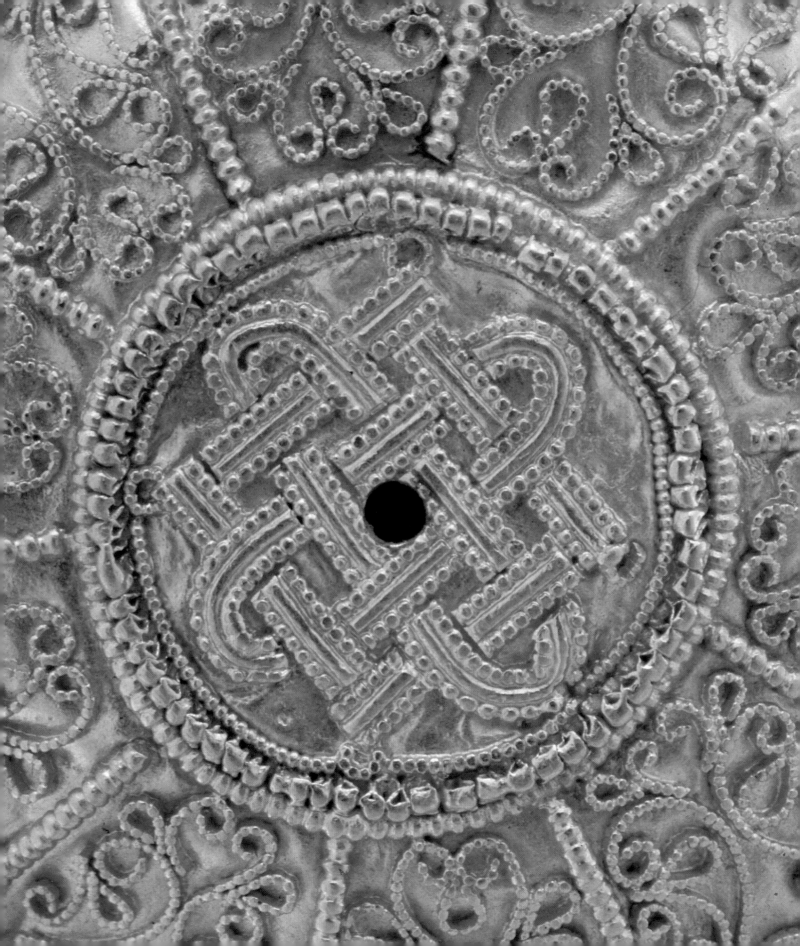

The filigree ornament of the sceptre-head setting is extremely fine work; the rich pattern, bent from very thin indented wire, was soldered onto the base plate. The chief motif is the palmette of heart-shaped leaves. A similar pattern occurs on quite a few objects of Hungarian origin, a fact supporting the theory that the setting was produced in this country. The filigree patterns of the gold objects found in the last century in the area of the basilica at Székesfehérvár are the most closely related to it—namely the patterns of tiny belt-ends, small plates, buttons, jewel fragments of unknown purpose and a miniature crown (Hungarian National Museum, Budapest). Unfortunately, researchers only came into possession of these objects a long time after they had been found; it can be surmised, nonetheless, that they originate from a royal tomb. A few years ago, at another royal seat, the palace of Esztergom, an ear-clip was found, the pendant of which, representing a turreted building, is adorned with similar filigree work, small enamel plates and pearls. Finally, we must point to a similarity, observed by researchers some time ago, between the filigree ornament of the sceptre-head and the cross-bands of the crown. The connection between the jewels found in royal burial places and in the palace area on the one hand and the royal insignia on the other clearly indicates that all these objects were made in a goldsmith's workshop of the royal court. Dating the existence of the workshop is aided by the Székesfehérvár fragments—including the tiny crown—which probably originate from the tomb of the child-king Ladislas III buried in 1205. The dating of the cross-bands of the crown between 1160 and 1180 and placing the Esztergom ear-clip into the same time-period also confirm the assumption that the royal workshop, which also produced the setting of the sceptre, operated towards the end of the twelfth century in Béla III's court. This is corroborated by the similarity of style between the patterns of the filigree-adorned objects and the border on the collar of the mantle. The Byzantinizing taste apparent in the almost exclusive use of filigree work and in purely ornamental decoration on objects connected with the sceptre, is typical of Béla III's environment. Yet another object indicative of the Court should be mentioned in connection with the sceptre. The front and back of the twelfth-century reliquary, which is similar to an apostolic cross, were ornamented with gold wire. Its sides, however, were decorated with gilded silver filigree only—just as the sceptre itself was made of two kinds of material. On the front, the motifs drawn in bended wire adorn the underplate at intervals. On the back, the small, heart-shaped palms made of thicker wire were arranged into bands similarly to those on the handle of the sceptre. The apostolic cross stands on a rock-crystal globe which is connected by hinged bands to the later, fourteenth-century foot. The reliquary—according to Deér the original oath-cross of the Hungarian kings—was taken along with other treasures to Salzburg in 1476. This was done by János Beckensloer Archbishop of Esztergom.

The overlay on the handle of the sceptre differs from the setting of the head; this is explained by the fact of silver being less soft and less flexible than gold wire.

The question remains why this club-shaped, Oriental sceptre, previously unknown in Europe and of an antique form, was made at the end of the twelfth century. The reply can be but hypothetical. Perhaps the crystal sphere had been a sceptre-head in a previous period, and the one we know today was only a restored setting.

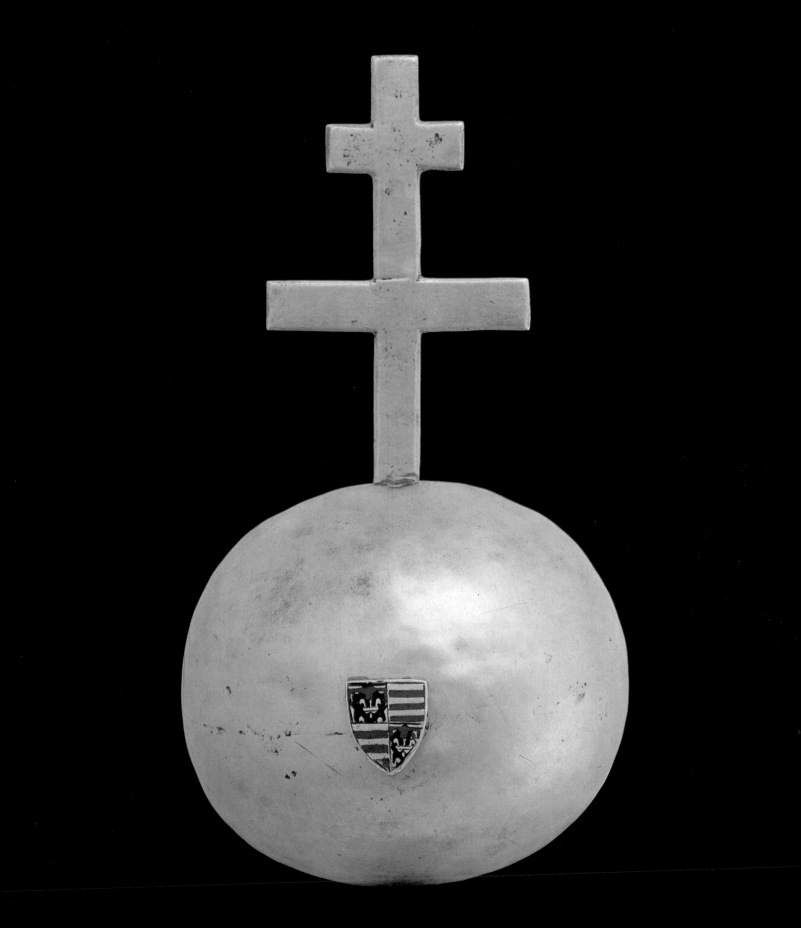

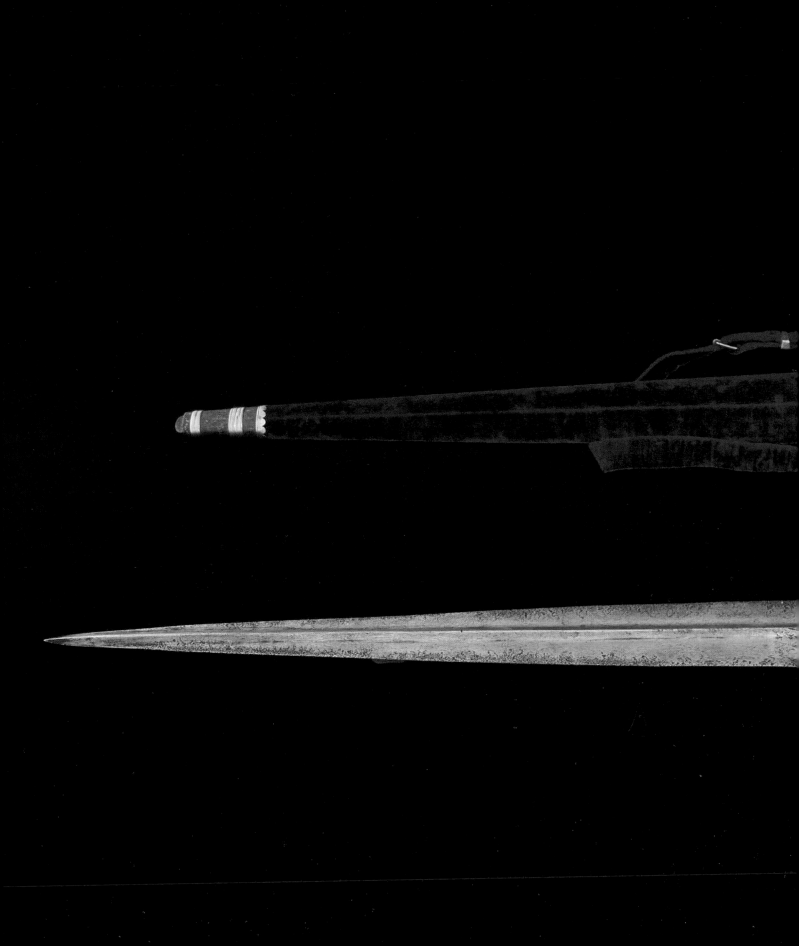

The Orb

An orb, held in St. Stephen's left hand, appears on the coronation mantle and, judging from coins and seals which have survived, it was used continuously throughout the Árpádian era. The gilded silver globe which has been preserved to this day was, however, only made in the fourteenth century, representing, as it does, the combined Hungarian and Anjou blazon *(fascé argent sur gueules,* resp. *fleur-de-lys-semés)*. Recent research (Vajay, Bak) permits a more exact dating, this differs from the heraldic device used exclusively by the Anjou kings of Hungary, and which is vertically divided in two fields. The quartered version on the orb is to be found only on Charles Robert's (Caroberto) denarius coin minted around 1301, probably in Zagreb, and of which only a few specimens now exist. Charles Robert was first crowned in 1301 with an emergency crown, as at the time, the traditional insignia were in the hands of his rival Wenceslas, King of Bohemia. The orb was certainly made for that occasion and this explains its unusually modest design. Also explained is its unique representation which emphasizes, in the midst of pretenders' struggles, the national origin of the person who had ordered it.

The apostolic cross on the top of the orb is also unique. The other regalia which have survived as well as the representations of the Hungarian kings up to the end of the twelfth century, are ornamented with a simple cross. The apostolic cross set in a heraldic shield—i.e. applied as an emblem—first appeared on the coins issued by King Béla III. No representation has been left from Béla III's reign which would directly support the contention that the orb had been ornamented with the apostolic cross. This, however, is highly probable if we consider that, in introducing the new emblem, the King followed the example of his foster-father, Manuel Comnenus. It was the latter who was depicted on his gold *solidus* coin with an orb surmounted by an apostolic cross. The addition to the orb of the apostolic cross can be proved for the century which followed, and the emblem ordered by Charles Robert, who stressed the Árpádian heritage, is a copy of it.

We do not know what happened to the former, original, orb. Mentioning the coronation, in 1290, of King Andrew III, the Austrian Rhymed Chronicle speaks of a "gold orb" *(aphel guldin)*. Even so, when young Wenceslas, according to the same chronicle, publicly appeared in royal robes in the summer of 1304, he held a sceptre in his right hand and St. Stephen's dexter in his left. As frequently occurred during later Hungarian history, the relic of our first holy king took the place of an emblem which had been lost. This is why the orb which was so simple in appearance could remain as part of the regalia even after the Holy Crown had passed into Charles Robert's possession, together with the other items used by his predecessors.

The Sword

The sword preserved among the regalia is the most modest piece in the set. It is a Venetian work from the beginning of the sixteenth century; there is an etched Renaissance ornament consisting of plant motifs and male masks at the upper end of its straight blade. At the top of the hilt, there is a flat pommel; the sword's broad cross-bar bends downwards. The velvet cover of its case, and even the copper mountings, were repeatedly renovated, the last time in the nineteenth century.

Since the sword figured in the coronation rites already in King Stephen's time, this object, much more modest than the contemporary ornamental weapons, could replace the emblem that had become lost earlier only on occasion. It is quite uncertain when it was included among the regalia. Since it looks worn, it must have been used as a weapon for quite a long time. The historical data dealing with the crown reveal nothing about it; and in the eighteenth century, when scientific investigations began, it was already one of the enshrined and much revered insignia.

AFTERWORD TO THE SECOND EDITION

When I was originally asked to co-author this book, only a few weeks had passed since the return to Hungary of the coronation regalia. Despite the fact that these relics had interested me ever since the beginning of my academic career and despite the fact that they had become even more mysterious and fascinating on account of their inaccessibility, I did not wish to take up my pen. "Now that we can, let us examine them afresh", I thought. Let us ignore the persuasive historical and insignia-centred accounts and compile a comprehensive description of the objects, a description based on careful study. In other words, let us draw up what in museum circles is termed a *catalogue raisonné*. Naturally, my reluctance did not stem from any underestimation of the need to inform the general public. My misgivings were bound up with chronology. Convinced as I was that experts should produce easily intelligible accounts based on balanced and considered analysis, I thought that technical appraisal would greatly help to introduce the regalia. However, as later events were to prove, I was too optimistic in this belief. True, examinations were begun but up to now at least, these have proved inconclusive. Restorer goldsmith Joachim Szvetnik and the authors of these lines gave a detailed account of the damage suffered by the crown over the centuries, and of the repairs which were carried out to it. In addition, Szvetnik also made exact and full measurements. Nevertheless, this work was but partly utilized. The most valuable observations of detail were made by David Buckton, who was fortunately uninfluenced by preconceived ideas deriving either from the history of insignia or from history generally. Indeed, Buckton was able to examine the two series of enamels on the crown from the disinterested standpoint of the art historian.

Systematic research has made more headway as far as the mantle is concerned. To facilitate its restoration, a routine examination of the material was made, the measurements and a description noted down, and analytical drawings produced. Katalin E. Nagy, one of the textile restorers who took part in this work, has given a short account of the results. Yet the historical evaluation of the findings thus obtained is still very important, and, without it, they are not particularly helpful. Incidentally, the mantle is not quite in the state shown by former pictures. When it was being examined, folds and pleats at the neck were undone and smoothed out. For this to happen, the collar had to be unstitched and the nineteenth-century violet silk lining folded back.

Apart from this, the coronation regalia are now seen differently from the point of view of science history. The various objects are no longer out of reach. In 1981, a select team of the most competent Hungarian and foreign specialists—art historians, those researching into textiles, experts on the goldsmith's art and on Byzantine studies—had the opportunity of inspecting the insignia during the course of a scientific conference. As well as the holding of this event, individual experts were also permitted to examine the objects in question. David Buckton was not the only one to inspect them. Mechtild Flury-Lemberg conducted her own survey and, at the request of the Hungarians, submitted a proposal that the mantle be restored. (This was followed by the comprehensive examination already described.) The conference was addressed by these two specialists, and Hermann Fillitz took the floor as well. Fillitz summarized the work of the late József Deér, the Hungarian scholar who wrote the most competent monograph about the crown, on the close relationship between the double reliquary cross originating from Esztergom (now at the Salzburg Cathedral Treasury), and the Hungarian sceptre. Regrettably, Hermann Fillitz's contributions did not take the form of a lecture. So, the insignia can now be examined, but the research to do with the crown has remained ambiguous in its conclusions. Frequently, the statements referring to the objects cannot be harmonized with the considerations suggested by historical analysis, and by postulates related to the history of the insignia. Deér was the last to treat the findings of the different disciplines according to their weight and significance, and it is not his fault if the objects, which he was unable to inspect personally, have not confirmed a number of his own ideas. I had hoped that the examinations undertaken would end this uncertainty once and for all, yet the overall picture gained from reports submitted at the conference and from research in general shows even more clearly than before that the starting point of researchers studying the objects themselves, on the one hand differs greatly from that of the historians. Factors which are of importance to the object-oriented investigator are not necessarily significant for the analyst whose approach is historical. Herein lies the reason for the extraordinarily varied picture we have of the insignia and of the crown in particular—a picture reflected by the current state of the research. Naturally, it is impossible to systematize and integrate the component parts of this picture. This is why the authors of the volume have made changes to the original text in places where new and noteworthy opinions have been expressed, and when these accord with analyses of the objects themselves. Alterations have also been made—and this mainly concerns the mantle—where examination has produced new, positive and illuminating observations. (Of course, in the bibliography, we have included all new works of a relevant and serious nature. We have even added to in other respects, while continuing to mention important contributions from earlier periods.) As a matter of fact, none of the recent findings has been of sufficient consequence to warrant substantial corrections. Indeed, my own additional research seems to confirm the view that the enamel plaques and the filigrees of the upper bands of the crown belong together and have Romanesque stylistic features. The Apostles and the abstract, decorative background, the peculiar *horror vacui* in the relationship between the elements of this, the isolation of the figures within the detail surrounding them—all are indicative of that particular variation of the special gold cloisonné enamel technique—the standard method of the age. The art associated with the name of Rogerus von Helmarshausen is essentially the same and, by means of the accessories and jewels greatly influences our image of that time. There the Byzantine impact is more immediate, while here it is more indirect and, for practical reasons, more indistinct. The same is true of the filigree consisting, on the crown, mainly of heart-shaped tendril-like decoration, while more complicated, symmetrical varieties indicative of Byzantine roots can be observed on the sceptre. However, in the light of our present knowledge, Byzantium can hardly be the direct source of the crown itself. Imitation occurred much earlier, and this is proved by the work to be seen on the masterpieces produced by European goldsmiths during the eleventh and twelfth centuries. Such decoration is certainly varied and frequently quite complicated, but always intended to fill space. Our objects represent the last stage of development in this particular direction before the appearance of the spiral filigree. At the same time, however, together with the enamel plaques, they exemplify the process the principal feature of which is the abandonment of the diversity of artistic and technical means of expression. The standardization which resulted led to contrasts not only with the art of the Ottonian era but also with that of Rogerus. This simpler treatment aptly characterizes numerous, and seemingly unrelated masterpieces produced in the mature Romanesque style by goldsmiths.

As for the Greek crown, the *corona graeca*, historians (Kerbl, Vajay) suggest a new, more exact and earlier date. On the basis of arguments which deserve attention, they claim that it was made during the second half of 1067—when the two Ducas brothers ruled jointly, with their mother acting as regent. Accordingly, the Byzantine co-regent portrayed on the crown and referred to by the abbreviation "KON" would not be Michael Ducas's young son Constantine, but, rather, his brother, Constantius and the Hungarian ruler not yet king, but heir apparent. In this case, the donation of the crown would have taken place during the long struggle for power between King Solomon of Hungary, who enjoyed the support of his relative the Emperor Henry IV, and Prince Géza. This struggle was interspersed with marriages and alliances, with Prince Géza utilizing his family connections (his sister married the youngest Ducas, Andronikos) in Byzantium—where intrigues between the two rivals were also carried on. The idea that the abbreviation could refer to both persons is by no means new. However, Kerbl produces additional historical arguments in support of an earlier dating. Kerbl's thesis raises the question as to what extent Moravcsik's classic analysis of the Hungarian King's Byzantine system of *tituli* should be revised, and whether it would have been possible for the Byzantine court to bestow in advance on a favoured prince the honour he strived for.

The interpretation of Byzantine imperial liturgy and, generally speaking, of the symbols of power as used in the Ducas court may be helped by the possibility of placing into a greater unit the enamel plaque mentioned—in more than one regard—in connection with the lower part of the Hungarian crown. This depicts the imperial couple's coronation by Christ (p. 42). As a matter of fact, four smaller plaques—mounted, secondarily, on the famous Khakhuli icon—also form part of the scene. These represent the depictions of saints on four square plates. In addition to St. George and St. Demetrius, who also appear in the image series of the crown, there is also the Archangel Michael holding the imperial crown (p. 23) and the Virgin Mary with the crown of the empress. These plaques undoubtedly form another symmetrical picture. The saints who, elsewhere, bring crowns of victory or bestow earthly power on individuals, are here depicted holding the characteristic male and female forms of the Byzantine crown, and are, at the same time, the patron saints of Michael Ducas and Empress Maria. Deér considered the coronation scene to be the work of the same goldsmith who made the Byzantine plaques of the Hungarian crown. This hypothesis, however, did not meet with a favourable response. The plaques of the crown are just a little more refined, and the same is indicated by the comparison of the plaques with identical themes representing militant saints. All of this is within limits narrow enough to indicate a close stylistic relationship.

Probably additional information can be found concerning the later vicissitudes of the objects from which, perhaps, conclusions may be drawn concerning their earlier history. It seems, for example, that Matthias II not only had a chest made for the insignia but also had the emblems repaired. In all likelihood, more happened to the crown than simply the mounting of a new sapphire. There are even indications that Matthias II not only had it copied but that he also had the mantle stitched onto a piece of new material. Anyway, in 1563, when Maximilian was crowned in Pozsony (now Bratislava, Czechoslovakia) the mantle was still ragged, at least according to an eyewitness account.

Naturally, the problems touched upon in this afterword indicate mainly the direction my own research has taken. I also believe that the repeated and detailed analysis of the pictures on the mantle is important. The results of such an analysis, together with a critical appraisal of the findings yielded by the technical examinations already mentioned, will be published in the second volume of *Insignia Regni Hungariae*. If all goes according to plan, the crown and the other metal objects will be dealt with in the third volume of the same series.

Budapest, Christmas 1985

ÉVA KOVÁCS

BIBLIOGRAPHY
OF THE LITERATURE DEALING WITH
THE CORONATION INSIGNIA

ALFÖLDY, A.: "Die Goldkanne von St. Maurice d'Agaune." *Zeitschrift für Schweizerische Archäologie und Kunstgeschichte* 10 (1948).

BALASSA, F.: *Casulae S. Stephani regis Hungariae vera imago et expositio.* Viennae, 1754.

BÁRÁNY-OBERSCHALL, M.: "Problémák a magyar Szent Korona körül." [Questions Related to the Holy Crown of Hungary]. *Antiquitas Hungarica I* (1947).

BÁRÁNY-OBERSCHALL, M.: "Localization of the Enamels in the Upper Hemisphere of the Holy Crown of Hungary." *The Art Bulletin* 31 (1949).

BÁRÁNY-OBERSCHALL, M.: "Die ungarische Stephanskrone im Lichte der neuesten Forschungen." *Südost-forschungen* 16 (1957).

BÁRÁNY-OBERSCHALL, M.: *Die Sankt Stephans-Krone und die Insignien des Königreiches Ungarn.* Vienna, 1961. 2nd edition: Vienna, 1974.

   Reviewed by BOGYAY, TH. in: *Byzantinische Zeitschrift* 56 (1963).

BARTONIEK, E.: *A magyar királykoronázások története* [The History of Coronations in Hungary]. Budapest, no date.

BENDA, K.–FÜGEDI, E.: *A magyar korona regénye* [The Romance of the Hungarian Crown]. Budapest, 1979. 2nd edition: Budapest, 1984.

BERTÉNYI, I.: *A magyar korona története* [The Story of the Hungarian Crown]. Budapest, 1978.

BOCK, F.: "Die ungarischen Reichsinsignien, VI.: Die Krone des hl. Stephan." *Mitteilungen der k.k. Central-Comission zur Erforschung und Erhaltung der Baudenkmale* 2 (1857).

BOCK, F.: *Die Kleinodien des Heiligen Römischen Reiches Deutscher Nation, nebst den Kroninsignien Böhmens, Ungarns und der Lombardei und ihrer formverwandten Parallelen.* Vienna, 1864.

BOCK, F.: *Die ungarische Königskrone "Corona Sancti Stephani" im Kronschatz der königlichen Schloßburg zu Ofen.* Aachen, 1896.

BODOR, I.: "A magyar korona legkorábbi ábrázolásai" [The Earliest Representations of the Hungarian Crown]. *Ars Hungarica* 1980/1.

BOECKLER, A.: "Die 'Stephanskrone'," in: SCHRAMM, P. E.: *Herrschaftszeichen und Staatssymbolik III.* Stuttgart, 1956.

BOGYAY, TH.: "Neuere Forschungen über die Stephanskrone." *Das Münster* 4 (1951).

BOGYAY, TH.: "A szent korona eredete. Kérdések és válaszok" [The Origins of the Holy Crown. Questions and Answers]. *Új Magyar Út* III (1952).

BOGYAY, TH.: "Problémák Szent István és koronája körül" [Problems Related to St. Stephen and His Crown]. *Új Látóhatár* 13/21 (1970).

BROWNING, R.: "A New Source on Byzantine-Hungarian Relations in the Twelfth Century." *Balkan Studies* 2 (1961).

CZOBOR, B.: *A magyar koronázási jelvények — Les insignes royaux de Hongrie.* Budapest, 1896.

CZOBOR, B.: "A magyar szent korona és a koronázási jelvények" [The Holy Crown of Hungary and the Coronation Insignia], in: FORSTER, GY.: *III. Béla emlékezete* (In Memoriam Béla III). Budapest, 1900.

DARKÓ, J.: *A Dukasz Mihály-féle korona célja és jelentősége* [The Purpose and Significance of the Michael Ducas Crown]. *Archivum Philologicum* 60 (1936).

DARKÓ, E.: Die ursprüngliche Bedeutung des unteren Teiles der ungarischen Heiligen Krone. *Seminarium Kondakovianum* 8 (1936).

DECSY, S.: *A magyar Szent Koronának és az ahoz tartozó tárgyaknak históriája* [History of the Holy Crown of Hungary and of the Related Objects]. Vienna, 1792.

DEÉR, J.: "Die Stephanskrone." *Atlantis* 21 (1949).

DEÉR, J.: "Der Globus des spätrömischen und des byzantinischen Kaisers, Symbol oder Insignie?" *Byzantinische Zeitschrift* 54 (1961).

DEÉR, J.: "Die byzantinisierenden Zellenschmelze der Linköping-Mitra und ihr Denkmalkreis Tortulae". Studien zu altchristlichen und byzantinischen Monumenten. *Römische Quartalschrift für christliche Altertumskunde und Kirchengeschichte* 30, Supplement (1966).

DEÉR, J.: *Die Heilige Krone Ungarns.* Vienna, 1966.

Reviewed by

    BAK, J.: in: *Jahrbücher für Geschichte Osteuropas* NF. 17 (1969);

    BOGYAY, TH.: in: *Byzantinische Zeitschrift* 61 (1968);

    FILLITZ, H.: in: *Kunstchronik,* Heft 1 (1972);

    LÁSZLÓ, GY.: in: *Századok* (1972);

    RENSING, T.: in: *Zeitschrift für Kunstgeschichte* 31 (1968);

    SCHRAMM, P. E.: in: *Zeitschrift für Schweizerische Archäologie und Kunstgeschichte* 25 (1968);

    VÁCZY, P.: in: *Magyar Hírlap* VII/226 (1974).

FALKE, O. von: "A Szent Korona" [The Holy Crown]. *Archaeologiai Értesítő* 43 (1929).

GEREVICH, T.: *Magyarország románkori emlékei* [Romanesque Relics of Hungary]. Budapest, 1938.

GYÖRFFY, GY.: "Mikor készülhetett a Szent Korona?" [When Could the Holy Crown Actually Have Been Made?] *Élet és Tudomány* 26/2 (1971).

GYÖRFFY, GY.: *István király és műve* [King Stephen and His Work]. Budapest, 1977.

HAMPEL, J.: "A magyar királyi korona és jelvényei" [The Hungarian Royal Crown and Its Insignia]. *Vasárnapi Újság* 27 (1880).

HAMPEL, J.: "A magyar Szent Korona" [The Holy Crown of Hungary]. *Archaeologiai Értesítő* 16 (1896).

HORÁNYI, E.: *De Sacra Corona Hungariae ac de regibus eadem redimitis commentarius.* Pestini, 1790.

HORVÁTH, J.: "Legrégibb magyarországi latin verses emlékeink" [The Oldest Latin Verses in Hungary]. *Irodalomtörténeti Értesítő* 60 (1956).

INSIGNIA REGNI HUNGARIAE I. *Studien zur Machtsymbolik des mittelalterlichen Ungarn.* (Lectures at the scientific session held on 22–24 September 1981 in the Hungarian National Museum.) Budapest, 1983.

IPOLYI, A.: "Beszámolója a korona vizsgálatára kiküldött bizottság munkájáról" [Account on the Work of the Commission Delegated for the Study of the Crown]. *A Magyar Tudományos Akadémia Értesítője* 14 (1880).

IPOLYI, A.: *A magyar Szent Korona és a koronázási jelvények története és műleírása* [History and Description of the Holy Crown of Hungary and the Coronation Insignia]. Budapest, 1886.

KARÁCSONYI, J.: "Hogyan lett Szent István koronája a magyar Szent Korona felső részévé?" [How did St. Stephen's Crown Become the Upper Part of the Holy Crown of Hungary?]. *Akadémiai Értekezések a történelmi tudományok köréből* 21/6 (1907).

KATONA, I.: *Dissertatio critica Stephani Katona presbyteri Strigoniensis in commentarium Alexii Horányi cl. reg. Piarum Scholarum de Sacra Hungariae Corona.* Budae, 1790.

KATONA, I.: *A magyar Szent Koronáról Doct. Decsy Sámueltől írt históriának meg-rostálása* [Examination of the History Written by Dr. Sámuel Decsy about the Holy Crown of Hungary]. Buda, 1793.

KELLEHER, P. J.: *The Holy Crown of Hungary.* Rome, 1951.

Reviewed by

    BÁRÁNY-OBERSCHALL, M.: in: *Corvina.* Ser. III, Vol. I (1952);

    BOGYAY, TH.: in: *Kunstchronik* 5 (1952);

BOGYAY, TH.: in: *Byzantinische Zeitschrift* 45 (1952);

DÖLGER, F.: in: *Historisches Jahrbuch der Görresgesellschaft* 75 (1954);

    FILLITZ, H.: in: *Mitteilungen des Institutes für Österreichische Geschichtsforschung* 63 (1955);

KERBL, R.: *Byzantinische Prinzessinnen in Ungarn zwischen 1050–1200 und ihr Einfluß auf das Arpaden-königreich. Dissertationen der Universität Wien* No. 143. Vienna, 1979.

KOLLER, J.: *De Sacra regni Ungariae Corona commentarius.* Quinqueecclesiis, 1800.

A KORONA KILENC ÉVSZÁZADA. *Történelmi források a magyar koronáról. Katona Tamás válogatásában, Györffy György tanulmányával* [Nine Centuries of the Crown. Historical Sources about the Hungarian Crown. Selected by Tamás Katona with an essay by György Györffy]. Budapest, 1979.

KOVÁCS, É.: "A magyar korona a legújabb kutatások tükrében" [The Crown of Hungary in the Light of Recent Research]. *Művészettörténeti Értesítő* 6 (1957).

KOVÁCS, É.: "Casula Sancti Stephani Regis." *Acta Historiae Artium* 5 (1958).

KOVÁCS, É.: *Romanesque Goldsmith's Art in Hungary.* Budapest, 1974.

KOVÁCS É.: "Les émaux 'latins' de la couronne de Hongrie." *Il medio oriente e l'occidente nell'arte del XIII secolo,* Atti del XXIV Congresso Internazionale di Storia dell'Arte, Bologna, 1982.

KOVÁCS É.: "Signum Crucis — Lignum Crucis (A régi magyar címer kettős keresztjének ábrázolásairól)" In: *Eszmetörténeti tanulmányok a magyar középkorról.* Memoria Saeculorum Hungariae 4. Budapest, 1984.

LÁSZLÓ, GY.: "Adatok a koronázási jogar régészeti mcgvilágításához" [Data to Clarify the Archaeological Aspects of the Coronation Sceptre]. *Szent István Emlékkönyv III.* Budapest, 1938.

MORAVCSIK, GY.: "A magyar Szent Korona görög feliratai" [The Greek Inscriptions on the Holy Crown of Hungary]. *Értekezések a Nyelv- és Széptudományi Osztály köréből* 25/5 (1935) and *Archivum Philologicum* 5 (1935).

MORAVCSIK, GY.: "A magyar Szent Korona a filológiai és történeti kutatások megvilágításában [The Holy Crown of Hungary in the Light of Philological and Historical Research]. *Szent István Emlékkönyv III.* Budapest, 1938.

Reviewed by

BÁRÁNY-OBERSCHALL, M.: in: *Folia Archaeologica* 1–2 (1939);

POLNER, Ö.: in: *Századok* 78 (1944).

E. NAGY, K.: "A koronázási palást restaurálásának előkészítése" [Preparing the Restoration of the Coronation mantle]. *Múzeumi Műtárgyvédelem* 12 (1983).

E. NAGY, K.: "An Account of the Preparations for the Coronation Mantle." *Conservation-Restoration of Church Textiles and Painted Flags. Investigation of Museums, Objects and Materials used in Conservation, Restoration.* Fourth International Restorer's Seminar. Volume 2. Budapest, 1984.

POLNER, Ö.: *A magyar Szent Korona felső részének eredetkérdése* [The Problem of the Origins of the Upper Part of the Holy Crown of Hungary]. Kolozsvár, 1943.

PULSZKY, K.: "A Szent Korona leírása" [Description of the Holy Crown]. *Archaeologiai Értesítő* 14 (1880).

RÉVAY, P.: *De Sacrae Coronae Regni Hungariae ortu, virtute, victoria, fortuna, annos ultra DC clarissimae brevis Commentarius Petri de Revva comitis comitatus de Turocz.* Augusta Vindelicorum, 1613.

ROSENBERG, M.: "Sacra Regni Hungariae Corona." *Der Cicerone* 9 (1917).

SACRALE GEWÄNDER DES MITTELALTERS. A catalogue. Munich, Bayerisches Nationalmuseum, 1955.

SCHMEIZEL, M.: *Commentatio historica de coronis tam antiquis quam modernis iisque regiies, speciatim de origine et fatis Sacrae, Angelicae et Apostolicae Regni Hungariae Coronae.* Jenae, 1713.

SCHRAMM, P. E.: *Herrschaftszeichen und Staatssymbolik* I. Stuttgart, 1954.

SCHWARZ, G.: *Initia religionis christianae inter Hungaros ecclesiae orientalis adserta.* Francofurti et Lipsiae, 1740.

SZÉKELY, GY.: Koronaküldések és királykreálások a X–XI. századi Európában [The bestowing of crowns and the making of kings in Europe in the 10th and 11th centuries]. *Századok* 1984.

SZILÁGYI, S.: "Révay Péter és a Szentkorona [Péter Révay and the Holy Crown]. *Értekezések a történelmi tudományok köréből* 5 (1876).

Tóth, E.: "Zur Ikonographie des ungarischen Krönungsmantels." *Folia Archaeologica* 24 (1973).

Uhlirz, M.: "Die Krone des hl. Stephan, des ersten Königs von Ungarn." *Veröffentlichungen des Instituts für österr. Geschichtsforschung* 14 (1951).

Reviewed by

Bogyay, Th.: in: *Byzantinische Zeitschrift* 45 (1952);

Deér, J.: in: *Historische Zeitschrift* 176 (1953).

Fillitz, H.: in: *Mitteilungen des Institutes für Österreichische Geschichtsforschung* 63 (1955).

Vajay, Sz.: "Az Árpád-kor uralmi szimbolikája" [The System of Regal Symbols of the Árpád House Era]. *Középkori Kútfőink Kritikus Kérdései.* Ed. J. Horváth and Gy. Székely. Budapest, 1974.

Vajay, Sz.: "La relique Stéphanoise dans la Sainte Couronne de Hongrie. *Acta Historiae Artium* 22 (1976).

Vajay, Sz.: "Corona Regia — Corona Regni — Sacra Corona." *Ungarn Jahrbuch* 7 (1976).

Vajay, Sz.: "Byzantinische Prinzessinnen in Ungarn". *Ungarn Jahrbuch* 10 (1979).

Varju, E.: "A Szent Korona" [The Holy Crown]. *Archaeologiai Értesítő* 39 (1920–22).

Wirth, P.: "Das bislang erste literarische Zeugnis für die Stephanskrone." *Byzantinische Zeitschrift* 53 (1960).

SIZES OF THE REGALIA

THE CROWN:
height: 17.9 cm
diameter: 20.4 and 21.5 cm, respectively
inner circumference: 63.6 cm

THE CORONATION MANTLE:
length: 136 cm
width: 284 cm
(*Band:*
length: 28 cm; width: 7 cm)

The collar:
width: 65 cm
height: 10 and 20 cm, respectively

THE SCEPTRE:
length: 37.5 cm

THE ORB:
height: 16.2 cm

THE SWORD:
length: 97.3 cm

Printed in Hungary, 1988
Kner printing House, Békéscsaba
CO 2538-h-8892